# DOCTOR JOHN

From the library of
## Danny Doyle
Raised on songs and stories

# DOCTOR JOHN

## CRUSADING DOCTOR & POLITICIAN

by Dr John O'Connell

POOLBEG

A Paperback Original
First published 1989 by
Poolbeg Press Ltd.
Knocksedan House,
Swords, Co. Dublin, Ireland.

The extract from *Ten Men Dead* by David Beresford is quoted
by kind permission of Grafton Books, London.

Proceedings of Dáil Eireann quoted by kind permission of the
Publications' Branch, Office of Public Works.

ISBN I 85371 025-3

Cover design by John Short
Typeset by Print-Forme
62 Santry Close, Dublin 9.
Printed by The Guernsey Press Ltd.,
Vale, Guernsey, Channel Islands.

# Acknowledgements

I would like to thank Brian Doolan and Peter Finnegan for reading the manuscript of this book and offering constructive suggestions. I am also grateful to Colette Cullen and Mary Boyle for their help in preparing the manuscript.

I would like to express my appreciation of all those who helped me in my political career, including Patrick Vickers, Paddy McNamara, Leo Martin and Harry Guerin.

*For My Family*

# CONTENTS

# Chapter 1

# A Start in Life and Medicine

Later, with hindsight, you could pick the texture loose. You could isolate threads and say this shouldn't have been so, or that. But at the time, it was all of a piece, functional, making sense.

Across each day ran the threads of religion; Mass in the morning, the family Rosary at night, predictable, comforting in their inevitability. Down through the weeks and months ran the expectations and the acceptance, holding it all together.

The prime focus in my father's life was his religion. He was a tall man, almost six foot, and very erect, probably because of the soldiering. He had been in the British Army, both in India, and, in the First World War, in France, coming home blinded in one eye, to chronic unemployment. There was a small pension of £2/8/- for financial support, and his religion for moral support.

Never having had much education, he taught himself to read and write, although to the day of his death, the full stop and he were strangers to each other. He could write a ten page letter with no full stop to halt the run of it from start to finish. He read a great deal, mostly religious books, lives of the saints, some of them aloud to my mother, who could barely read at all.

Fasting twice a week and commonly wearing a hair shirt, it was my father who orchestrated our religious life, who made sure we were up early in the morning to go to Mass and home in time for the family rosary; in a sense he was the guiding figure in the household, because my mother invariably deferred to him. What he said, went.

Not that he ever said very much. A quiet man, except in sporadic fits of temper which came without warning and left him filled with remorse. When it happened, my mother was the target, and the aftermath saw him bringing her little paper bags with a quarter pound of sweets in them as peace offerings.

I seem to remember that he had drinking bouts at some stage when I was very young, but about the time he passed his fortieth birthday, he gave up drink altogether and never touched it again, probably as part of his religious thinking.

My mother was a thin little woman, kind, attentive and a worrier. She had an infinite capacity for worry — about us, our education, our health — coupled with an infinite capacity for serving other people. She respected, even, I suspect, feared my father. In my younger days, I thought there might have been friction there, but as I grew older, I became aware that he was very attentive to her: he encouraged her to try to read, and used to read his religious books to her.

She had a disability : one leg was permanently swollen as the result of a puerperal infection. Even as a child, I was conscious of her embarrassment over that leg. She was always looking for elastic stockings to try to conceal and reduce the swelling. Later, when she was completely disabled and almost bedfast, my father would carry her downstairs a few times in the night to let her use the toilet, and was very devoted to her.

I started off in Aungier Street, Number 73 — now a derelict site opposite the birthplace of the poet Thomas Moore. Dublin in the early thirties was seething with tenements and my mother would recount how we had moved from Bride Street to York Street and then to Aungier Street where I was born. There, we had what was known as a "two pair back" — two rooms at the back of a tenement house. When I was still a toddler, we moved out to a Dublin Corporation house in Joyce Road, Drumcondra. It was a two-bedroomed corner house in what I recall as a singularly happy neighbourhood. Two bedrooms. One for my parents, one for the children. At that time, there were six of us, and Sylvie, the eldest, was slowly dying from rheumatic heart disease. In our tiny room were three beds. Sylvie slept in his own bed. My two brothers shared another while I slept in the third bed with my two sisters.

Today, rheumatic fever is a fast disappearing disease, mainly because of improved nutrition and better heating in houses. Then, it was part of life to know that Sylvie, coming up to sixteen, was dying, not in much pain, but breathless, breathless all the time.

It was accepted.

Having a mortally sick child in the house was not peculiar to us. If it happened, the options were simple. You nursed him, (in our case, this was done by my mother) you prepared the room for the doctor's brief visits, and you waited for the inevitable. Of course, not all aspects of the sickness were accepted. My father often talked bitterly of the way we were treated by doctors. The brusque manner. The lack of explanation. They came and went without a comment, and there was little you could change about it, because doctors were kings in their own area and talking back or questioning was just not done.

Sylvie died when I was four, and one of my earliest memories is the horror of being accidentally locked in for a few minutes with the dead body. Curious, the long-term stamp such an incident leaves on the mind. The sensation and the fear stayed with me for years, so that even when I was a doctor working in the States, doing post-mortems on my own, that frightened feeling would overwhelm me.

In one way, I suppose I had little childhood, in the sense we use the phrase today; little time just to be irresponsible and to play. Like many of my generation in Dublin, I was brought up in an atmosphere of strict discipline, of all-pervasive authority, unquestioned and infallible, although not based on violence, but on expectation.

You were expected to ask permission before you went out. You were expected not to stray too far. Expected to report on time for the family rosary, to do your tasks. Expected not to break or damage things. Expected, most of all, to understand the sacrifices being made by your parents in order to keep the family afloat, and not to do anything which might interfere with that effort. Gentle but ruthless expectations you built into your own thinking and your own attitude to life.

3

We made a quiet, obedient group of children. Once only was a hand raised to me, and that was when I arrived home late for tea having forgotten to let them know where I was going. When I came back, I was slapped out of fear and relief by my mother — under my father's direction!

For many families in our area at the time, money was the major problem. In 1939, for example, we had about £2 and 8 shillings a week to cover everything. Coping on such a small income was difficult, but it had to be done. If there were alternatives, my parents did not accept that they applied to us. Once, I recall, the local priest came to see my father and they talked for a long time in low voices behind a closed door before parting civilly on the doorstep. My father came back to the kitchen.

"He said he could organise some help for us," he said to my mother. "Get us clothes other people would give him".

"What did you say?"

"I just told him thank you, but we would accept charity under no circumstances". A nod from my mother, and that was the end of the story. We coped by various means. There was the half-hour trudge from Drumcondra down to Kennedy's bakery in Parnell Street for broken loaves, which came a lot cheaper than ordinary loaves — a trudge you didn't really resent, since one half of the journey was made blissful by a mouthful of warm broken bread. There were the visits to Rourke's bakery for four-day old bread, collected in a pillow case. On one of those visits, we were watched incredulously by a group of what we called "posh" people. My mother's embarrassment as she fought to get the bread into the pillow case was painful to watch, and the memory of it stayed with me for years.

Once or twice, items slipped past my father's "no charity" rule, and I remember once having a pair of girl's shoes with slightly higher than normal heels. Today, they'd be fashionable. Then, they made me cringe with shame. Not that I ever mentioned it at home, though I spent some hours trying to remove part of the heel. Complaining at home would never have occurred to any of us, even when later we were jeered at school for our clothes, since my mother was somewhat erratic in her choice of colours for patches, and would happily sew a green patch on brown trousers.

Even if they had time to listen to you, it was not the sort of complaint you brought to your parents. You accepted it and got on with the day's chores.

The day began early — at half past six. Somebody went for a penn'orth of milk from the milkman, who toured the neighbourhood with his big cans of milk using a horse and dray. Milk — and porridge. The table was a drop-leaf piece of wood over the bath in the kitchen, common to many Dublin houses of the time. Perhaps because it wasn't a proper table, I can never remember meals as sit-down, sociable events. They were quickly snatched. Then there was school, and afterwards, there was homework. Little time for sport or games, because studying took up so much of our time. This arose because of my parents' conviction that only through education could we escape the limitations of their lives.

My mother was rigidly clear on this point. She herself had never been to school, and could barely write. Even her own name was a difficulty for her to put down on paper, but she decided early on that none of the young O'Connells was going to be able to say THAT in later life about himself or herself. Not only were we going to go to school — we were going to the best schools. To that end, she saw the Head in St Vincent's secondary school in Glasnevin. It was an orphanage, but it took day pupils as well. At her interview with Brother Cluskey, the Head, she made a bargain with him. All of her children would have totally free secondary education, on one condition — that each of them always got first place in the class. Which, in due course, we did, accepting without question the importance of schoolwork and home study.

There was constant encouragement at home. My father wasn't able to help us much with the books, but his attitude helped.

"You'll do it", he'd say calmly. "You'll get that exam, I know you have it in you."

Today, they would say he was making over-achievers of us, but it wouldn't be true. He never forced any of us, or bullied us.

There was just the quiet expectation that we would do well - an expectation that gradually became internalised in us, so that to this day, faced with something new, I find myself thinking, "Yes, you can handle this, of course you can."

The regime was not consistent, of course. What family regime ever is? My mother was strong on treats, always trying to find some way of giving us a little boost, and one regular treat was letting us all off school a week earlier than the regular holidays. For some reason, she felt that we should have that little extra break. The only problem was that we had always studied so hard that there were often prizes for us on the final day, and we were seldom there to collect them.

We were a most united family. Sylvie, who died when I was four, was two or three years older than Sammy. Then came my brother Pat. Next, Kathleen, who was two years older than me, and with her I had an especially close relationship. She seemed to take me everywhere with her. My youngest sister Pam was three years younger than me.

On the debit side, there was the fact that we were always hungry, and that we saw some foods — like meat — so rarely that they scarcely featured in our diet. Rationing still applied to some foods but those who were "in the know" managed to live well. I can still recall being hungry all day long. For us, though, a pennyworth of chips for dinner was a treat, and a cream cake a cause for celebration. With hunger went the threat of illness. A threat that was realised in the case of Kathleen. She was fourteen when glands in her neck swelled.

I was the runner at that stage, and I was sent to fetch Dr O'Donnell, the local GP, while the preparations went on at home — getting the room straight, laying out the basin of water and the towel and soap.

"She'll be all right," he said in his abrupt way. "Get her down to the hospital."

That was the Mater Hospital. They removed the glands that caused the disease and in the process spread the infection. The disease recurred in a localised area, in her case the hip, and just went to work. She had a limp from then on. Of course, at that time, nobody ever admitted to having TB. Whatever else you had, you didn't have TB.

Nobody in your family, seed, breed or generation, had TB.

I remember a priest came to the house and was talking about it with my parents, and he said "As long as you didn't have it and your husband didn't have it, you'll be alright." Which made no sense at all, but people wanted to tell themselves that everything would be all right, even though we knew and instinctively accepted that it would not.

For Kathleen there were the visits as an outpatient to the Mater Hospital, (where I was later to serve as a doctor,) queueing for hours and hours on long benches like church pews, moving in tired sideways motion to fill the gap left by your neighbour's lurch to the left, the gap running down like a slow wave through the pews and the people to the last seated person, or to the man waiting in line to sit down, the smells of close-packed people eddying with the movement. All of it supervised by authoritarian nuns. At the end of it, the journey home with the bottle of medicine.

Some time after this, my mother heard of a famous TB specialist, and got my sister along to see him. He admitted her into the TB unit in the Richmond. He was under the misapprehension that we had money, and when he found out that we hadn't, she was simply transferred in the dead of night to the south Dublin Union in Rialto, successor to the poorhouse. There was no qualified nursing care whatever there, merely paupers who served as attendants. Nor were we notified. On the next visit to the Richmond Hospital we were simply informed that she was no longer there, and told where she was, in the South Dublin Union, which was just about the worst thing, the most humiliating thing that could happen to a Dubliner.

My father was outraged. He confronted the TB Medical Officer, in the TB clinic in Charles Street, and raged at him.

"I told him they had no right to treat anybody like this," he said, adding, with a reference to the war then being fought, "I said to him, 'The swastika isn't flying over Dublin yet, you know.'"

After that, she was taken to Crooksling Sanatorium and the

Sunday visits began. Weird, those Sunday visits. All the girls in bed in those open huts without windows, with the wind whistling around them, and all looking healthy because of the unreal tubercular glow they had. Each week, four or five missing — dead. Each week my sister, thin and blonde and pretty with flushed cheeks, telling us stories of the week's deaths, and asking for new novenas. All the time, new novenas. For her, the days ceased to be days of the week, and became just occasions for saying the rosary, and time was gathered into novenas of desperate hope.

The great paradox of my childhood was that on the one hand, you accepted illness and death as part of the pattern, but on the other, you were filled with hope in the power of prayer. Kathleen did novena after novena. She was nearly sixteen.

I will always remember that towards the end, she wanted ice so badly. She was feverish in the last stages, having what they called the "night sweats."

She lost weight by the stone in the night sweats, became a gaunt figure, and she was in agony for ice. But where could we get ice?

The fact is that by the time I was grown up, our family had been halved. Two children, Sylvie and Kathleen, were dead, indirect victims of poverty, and a third, Sammy, died abroad. Sammy was the second eldest, and there had been some talk of his joining the Jesuits — talk which, oddly enough, brought hostility from my father, who, although a most religious man, didn't want Sammy to be a Jesuit. However, Sammy in the meantime developed an interest in flying, and joined the RAF at seventeen, much to my mother's grief, because she hated to see him going away. He used to write home regularly, and the letters were always a sort of celebration. We read them aloud.

One week during the war, he wrote about a pilot friend of his who'd been shot down over the North Sea. The following week, we got a notice that Sammy himself was reported missing. The painful irony was that just at this time there was a news blackout and censorship introduced into Britain and so letters from the soldiers were being delayed, with the result that a few days after the notification that he was missing in action (believed killed) we got a letter from Sammy to say he was coming home. Of course, this filled us with hope and confusion, and my father queried it, writing to anybody he thought might be able to get us news. For a long, long time, my mother and father both refused to admit that the notification might be right. They used to go down to the trains at Westland Row and to the North Wall when the soldiers were coming in, in the hope that he'd be among them, and they would come back silent and strained.

They went down a great many times, until eventually, we got a letter saying his belongings were being sent on, and that was the end of the hoping. It was another event to be accepted and prayed into its context.

Just when I began to think about being a doctor, I cannot now recall. I know the idea was fully formed when I was half way through secondary school, because I spent whatever pennies I had on medical books from the tables outside the second hand bookshops on the quays — books of which my parents evidently disapproved, because they would go missing on me. I would never ask what happened to them, because of a feeling of embarrassment — perhaps I should never have had them at all? But then, certain things were never discussed at home. My ambition to be a doctor, for one thing. I never mentioned it, all through school. Neither parent would have understood or approved.

Father in particular believed the Civil Service was the only place, and he thought that should be my ambition; to get into the Civil Service. We would discuss it at length, but never mention alternatives, so when I left school at seventeen, I joined the Civil Service, and all I heard for weeks from senior staff was "You've got only two things to worry about here, your pension and your holidays." I was in the Civil Service Commission checking applications for Civil Service examinations. While everyone was very courteous to me, after a week I knew it would drive me mad.

The routine of it, and the senseless bureaucracy. Of course, I turned the existing system on its end in double quick time by signing my name instead of a squiggle on the end of any letter I sent out, which was unheard of at that period. Within weeks, people getting those letters had copped on that there was SOMEONE up there in the Department with a name, and I was getting letters from all over the country. That didn't bother me — I went a step further and always wrote "Dear Mr X or Y" instead of "Dear Sir" which I thought was very impersonal, but there was a distinct feeling that you didn't do That Sort of Thing in the Civil Service.

Of course, in recent times, the accepted wisdom is that this is precisely what SHOULD happen, but at that time it was very strange.

The only advantage I could see attached to Civil Service employment was that I had some real money in my pocket for the first time, and I set to saving for my medical fees, told my parents what I planned, and after six months resigned.

All of which sounds easier than in fact it was. I was literally afraid to reveal my plans to other people, for fear they would think I was too presumptuous. My fears were not groundless, for when I went to the local doctor for a necessary reference, he refused it. I had gone to his great imposing house to make the request, and he looked me up and down when I explained what I planned to do.

"The College of Surgeons," he said crushingly, "is for doctors and doctors' sons."

I went away without my reference, but with my determination still intact. Some time later I was bringing a friend to see another medical man, a Dr Baker, and I took a leap in the dark and asked this doctor for a reference. He was quite fascinated by the idea of my trying for medical school and was delighted to serve as my referee. By co-incidence, years later, I met him in my finals. He didn't remember me. I didn't remind him. I just looked at him and said a mental "thank you."

Armed with his reference, I got the syllabus, sent my application, paid my fees, and was committed to medicine, with no notion of what it would be like or whether I would be a success. For once, even my father's encouraging optimism failed. He couldn't say "I know you'll do well," because he didn't know. He clearly thought I was mad to throw up a secure pensionable job, such as had eluded him all his life, for a pipe-dream. For me, it was all a mystery and a challenge. Inevitably, it was a challenge that was going to cost money. Where to get the cash to pay my way was the first practical problem.

There was a fashion, not too long ago, for the back of a book's jacket to read like an eccentric's curriculum vitae. The author's face would stare out wisely over a paragraph into which, pressed down and flowing over, were packed the jobs of his or her past life: "Has been a lumberjack, short-order cook, garbage man, Carthusian monk and zither-restorer." My potted biography would read - "has been a bookie's clerk, fluorescent light installer, waiter, storeman, newspaper editor, doctor — and politician." And that's leaving out a few...

My time as a bookie's clerk began while I was at school. I was fourteen and a half when some friend offered me the chance of the work, and I took it. It entailed taking down the bets called out by the bookie, and the numbers of the tickets, understanding such terms as "six to four the field" and "two to one bar" and then totting up how much was in the bag and how much was to be paid out. The bookie's clerk is the one who points out to the bookmaker if he stands to lose too much on a particular horse or dog, or that a change of odds is indicated.

I used to go every Monday and Friday to Dundalk Dog Track with my bookie, Billy Eastwood, on the train, racing from school to Amiens Street, staying overnight in Dundalk and coming back the following morning. I was always late for school on the mornings after Dundalk, but I got away with it in the early stages, although later, when I was about sixteen, the bookie wanted me to do more and more point-to-point meetings for him, and I ran into real conflict at school over that.

"You just can't do it and expect to do well in your studies," Brother O'Driscoll told me, very seriously. "You've got to choose."

The dingy, limp, orange ten shilling notes I earned were handed up at home to make the family struggle less grinding. The bookies were decent people. Good people. I liked them and their company. They had a tough enough life, some of them just managing to get by, but they had time to be protective of the

11

teenager.

"Watch it," they'd say to one of their number who would be launched on a dirty joke. "Watch it. The kid's listening." They were to remember me many years later when Dublin bookmaker Sonny Molloy on their behalf sent me a telegram of congratulations on my first election to the Dáil in 1965. Again in 1979, bookmaker Terry Rogers publicly put on record his full support for me in a newspaper advertisement during my election campaign for the European Parliament.

Even though I could no longer do the racing work, it was obvious, when first I entered the College of Surgeons on my first day there, that I should have to find some way of making money which did not take me away from Dublin. If I had stayed at home, I could, of course, have lived off my parents, but for me, that was never a real possibility. My parents fought with me when I told them I was joining three other fellows in a flat in Grove Park, Rathmines, and that grieved me, but I had made up my mind, and I'm hard to shift once my mind is made up. I still visited them once a week, but for the first time, I was living away from home. Carrying much of home with me, of course. Going to Mass every morning, the only boy in the flat to do so, and being jeered at for it. I was learning to pick some of the threads of my upbringing apart and learning to decide for myself what was important and what needed to be left behind with childhood.

The first day in College was a nightmare. To this day I find the College of Surgeons an imposing building. Then, it seemed massive, stiff with fat columns and enlivened (or perhaps I should say deadened) by the busts of famous medical men. The smell of formaldehyde from the anatomy room permeated the entire College. The College Registrar, Professor Norman Rae turned out to be an old, slightly bent man with a wry sense of humour.

What I remember best, though, is the conversation I overheard in the afternoon, between two students, four or five years older than I was.

"Camberwell's turned into a chronic," one of them said. "He'll be here repeating exams until his father's money runs out."

"Or his father's patience."

"No, the money'll go first. Old man Camberwell has a lot of patience when it comes to making Son and Heir into his successor in medicine."

"Wonder if he knows how Son and Heir spends his time?"

"In Neary's pub you mean?"

"Neary's or Roberts' Cafe. Once you begin spending time in either of them, you might as well have "chronic" branded on your forehead."

End of conversation. And the beginning of my determination that, no matter what anybody said about "broadening yourself as a person by involving yourself in social activities", I would never go drinking, playing games, join societies, or socialise in any way which might interfere with my work, because I was different. If one of the young men who started the course with me on that October morning failed an exam, it was "What a shame — better luck in September." If I failed, it was disaster. Furthermore, it was a lonely disaster. I had thrown up my good pensionable job, left home, and invested every penny I had — for what? I had, as yet, no idea. True, I had a good Leaving Cert under my belt, but I was not naive enough to believe that studying medicine was just an extension of Secondary school. For all I knew, exams here did not depend on how hard you studied. "For doctors and doctors' sons ..." The words of my GP echoed in my ears. Maybe doctors' sons would have some sophisticated knowledge which I, without their background, would lack.

Fortunately, the practical problems of survival impinged on me very quickly and saved me from too much fearful introspection. A friend mentioned a job going as a fluorescent light installer, and I went along to try my hand at it. What I found was that the early lectures in the pre-med course might have been designed to make a fluorescent light installer out of me, covering, as they did, subjects like the basics of electrical theory. The suppliers of the fluorescent lights took me on and showed me how to put the fittings up, and off I went with a bundle of them under my arm. A girl in a tobacconist's shop

13

around the corner from the College agreed to reserve the space behind the shop door for my lights, so, each morning, I set off for the College, lights under my arm, and parked them. The moment morning lectures were over, I retrieved the lights and went in search of customers. Publicans were, I discovered, the best marks.

At this time fluorescent lighting was new, and lighting itself was becoming more important. It was easy enough to walk into a pub and show the owner how dirty and inadequate his existing lights were, and how cheap and efficient the new fluorescent strips.

"You get as much light from a forty watt strip as you would from a two hundred watt bulb ..."

Bits of my own sales-talk, remembered. I did not have a set patter, and so the first few moments were full of stammers and dithers. To this day, I hate the first contact, the introducing of myself to people who don't know me. Back then, it was something to be nerved up to and done quickly, and at least the strips were obviously better, in most cases, than the existing lighting system. Once an agreement had been made, I climbed up and fitted the lights, my skin crawling with the certainty that one of the upturned, curious faces surrounding the bar belonged to an electrician who could do it better and faster and would eventually say so. Then it was collect the money and get back to College as fast as possible. Not that this was always easy. In one bar in Wexford Street, I fitted my lights and asked for my money, and the man behind the bar smiled and said no, he'd changed his mind and would pay me half what we had agreed.

I went cold all over. Not only would I have no profit, but I'd have to pay for the lights myself, for how could I force him? I stood, explaining to his implacably smiling face that we had made a bargain, and suddenly two big men who had been silently watching me work, stood up and came close to us.

"He did a good job for you," one of them said. "Pay him."

"Pay him or we don't drink here any more," said the other. The landlord counted out the correct money without a word, and I left, mumbling thanks to my two champions. Big, quiet men I never saw before or since.

14

If publicans, generally, were good marks for my salesmanship, there were others who were more difficult. One of Dublin's biggest department stores was impressed by the lights, but wanted to test them for a month in their basement.

"Install eight lights and leave them for a month," a Mr Roche of Roches Stores said. "And if we're happy with them, you'll have the order for the entire store."

It was an order I never got, though, because the suppliers of the lights refused the trial, and I had no capital to buy and lend the lights myself.

Another order I never got was Hector Gray's.

"You're the best salesman I've ever met," he said, when I showed him the lights and talked about them, and he told me that when he opened his second and third stores, I would supply the lights. In fact the deal was never completed, although I now forget why not.

By selling the lights, I could afford to pay my share of the rent of our shared flat, and also to contribute to its running. The four of us — Tom Stack, Jimmy Carroll, Tommy Cairns and myself — took it turn and turn about to buy and cook the food. I remember the first time I was bursar, I carefully unpacked my purchases under the eye of Tom Stack. He came nearer and nearer to the table. When it was all unpacked, there was a small silence.

"Jesus," he said softly, "is that the week's food?"

"Yes," I said.

"You shouldn't be let out on your own without a keeper," he said unkindly. He was right, of course. I had been most uneconomical and had bought all the wrong things. I had absolutely no sense of budget at all. But I learned. I learned largely because the fear of either being thrown out of the group of people sharing the flat, or worse still, being thrown out of the flat itself, was so big that it overshadowed everything else.

There was the time coming up to the end of the first term when the other lads had already gone home and I was in the house on my own, except for a teacher and his wife, who were staying downstairs. I had a friend, Frank Burke from Drumcondra, who was always threatening to match me up with a girl, and one night, he arrived with two — one for himself, and one for me. What he hadn't realised was that the landlady's daughter was a one-woman League of Decency who prowled constantly on the off-chance that she might spot one of the tenants taking a girl up to his room; a dire crime, this, resulting in expulsion not just for the offender, but also for his legitimate flatmates.

Frank arrived this night, overpoweringly cheerful, and propelled a pretty stranger up the stairs towards me.

I gave her a timorous welcome, and she had just stepped behind me to hang her coat up when the landlady's daughter appeared beside Frank at the bottom of the stairs.

"And just what carousing is going on here?" she demanded, in a voice that put your teeth on edge. Frank was dumbstruck.

"*Women* are not permitted in this house. No tenant is allowed to bring *women* in here".

Frank's girlfriend blushed. The landlady's daughter had a way of inflecting "Women" which made it like a four letter word.

"I wasn't staying," he said, with some dignity. "I just came to give John a message."

"Be on your way, then," said the landlady's daughter.

Frank was on his way. The landlady's daughter favoured me with a glance full of menace, and disappeared.

I retreated into the flat, to find it occupied by the strange girl, who had heard the exchange downstairs, didn't know me from a hole in the wall, and realised that short of braving the dragon, she was stuck here for the night. She looked at me. I looked at her.

"I'm sorry," I whispered lamely.

"It's not your fault," she said, fairmindedly, but without much enthusiasm. For a long time (in order to let the landlady's daughter settle, like tealeaves) we sat there in silence, and then we spent the entire night talking, awaiting the dawn and the departure of the landlady and her daughter for Mass, so that this poor wisp of a girl could leave for her work. As soon as the landlady and her daughter left the house, I ushered the strange girl down the stairs to the tram at Portobello Bridge promising to make further contact, but it never materialised.

At the time, in an effort to be sociable, I even went dancing, although this didn't come easy to me, probably due to lack of confidence. The only time I ever managed to acquit myself with any aplomb at all was when I was going out for a while with a professional dancer. Under her whispered commands, I was able to glide around the floor, but using my own initiative I simply blundered from point A to point B.

What social life I had consisted of going to the odd football match in Croke Park, seeing such films as "Gone with the Wind" or "The Best Years of our Lives", and occasionally having a meal out at the Dog and Waffle, South Richmond Street. It was sparse, at best, and yet I have a recollection of myself at that time as being almost constantly in love. With different girls, and for short periods. Of course the advice columns would say it was "just infatuation," but I'm loth to dismiss it like that. It's very beautiful, this magical thing that happens when you meet someone and for a time, even a short time, you see in her everything a human being should be.

Apart from the scattered occasions when I went dancing or to the pictures, my first years at college were a constant slog. Nor did it end with term-end. I finished term in the summer on a Friday, and on the Saturday I went to the Isle of Man to get a summer job. I persuaded another friend to come with me, and on that Saturday, we found ourselves homeless, jobless and very nearly moneyless on the island.

"How much have you got?" I asked him. I had no money at all. He showed me.

"OK," I said. "Let's spend it on a game of snooker while we think what to do next."

"You're mad," he said, and handed over the money. Once the snooker game was over, we found a lodging house and persuaded the landlady to take us in for the night.

"We don't have any money," I said. "But we'll have a job by tomorrow night."

I had, too. As a storeman in the holiday camp. It was slavery. Up at work at 6 a.m., finish at 6 p.m. One of my jobs was to be driven on a truck out to the potato fields where the driver would park to read the racing page of his paper and I would dig, clean and pack into sacks the potatoes for that day's lunch. Anything up to six sackfuls might be needed.

In the stores, it was a case of dragging and hauling great sacks of flour and other foodstuffs out for use. Four pounds and your keep. It was the "your keep" bit which provoked me into my first attempt at militant action. Our quarters were filthy, and the food disgusting. Six of us went down one night and demanded that they clean things up. We succeeded, too. They were quite amenable. Of course, from my point of view, with next year's fees and food to be taken care of, £4 was not enough, so I took another job to supplement the first, working as a waiter from 7.30 p.m. until 12 midnight. For that, I was paid no wages at all, but depended on tips. The problem was that someone from Dublin might see you, in your distinctive brown denim work-suit. Perhaps I was unduly sensitive, but I dreaded that with a constant, low-level, nagging fear.

In the whole of the season, we had two days off. On one of them, I took a bus tour around the island, and, probably because I was so tired, and had seen nothing up to then but the behind-the-scenes aspect of it, the place had a shattering impact on me. I thought it beautiful, especially Port Erin and Port St Mary from where you could see the Mountains of Mourne. Years later I fulfilled an ambition to go back there, as a tourist, and was bitterly disappointed. It did not come up to my expectations, but then it's always a mistake to go back.

After that spell, it was a return to Dublin and my own tiny flat. One of the others had failed his exam, another had gone somewhere else for a year, and so the group of four broke up. I had learned a lot from the three fellows. They had broadened my views on a good many things, poked a little fun at me, and helped me to be less self-conscious about my background. But it was good to be on my own.

I had friends, of course, one in particular, Roy Wilson, from the North of Ireland who reckoned that my feverish attention to my books just might be catching. He invited me to stay with him and we would work together. He appeared to be very wealthy, having inherited a business (something to do with

18

buying sacks from the farmers, and selling them back to the millers) and he impressed on me that the conditions for study would be second to none. He also pressed a fifty pound note — "For expenses" into my hand; the first I had ever seen. So off we set, and we lived for some weeks in his palatial home in Magherafelt north of the Border, during which time he developed an increasingly large need for company. One day, he announced that he had to visit a friend who was a lecturer at Magee College, Derry and we set off together in his luxurious car, on the back seat of which he had a case of beer.

Arriving, we were shown to the lecturer's room to await him. Somewhere along the line, we had picked up Roy's fiancée, and we sat, all three of us, with the case of beer and waited. They decided they had to have a beer each — I didn't drink. No bottle opener. Simple, my friend said, and smashed two bottles open against the carved fireplace. Drank. Smashed two more. Drank. Smashed...

After a while, the lecturer still had not come, but my two friends' talk was rising in decibel count by the minute, and the foam from the bottles smashing off the fireplace was flowing in a scummy stream under the door and down the stairs outside. I began to dread the inevitable.

It came. Knock Knock on the door. A housekeeper, pink in the face with outrage over the noise and the stream of beer. Once the door was opened, her face darkened to puce when she saw that the source of the brown stream outside the door was extensive and growing every minute. She began calling for the President of the College. My friend panicked.

"Grab that end John", he said, snatching at the other end of the case of beer, now depleted, but not empty by any means. I obeyed orders, and we set off down the stairs. Unfortunately, we set off at some speed, and the stairs had a light coating of beer foam on them, and we both lost our grip on the case of beer which went crashing down the steps in an earsplitting cacophony of breaking box, smashing bottles and a muddle of flying beer bubbles and brown liquor.

"Run for the car," Roy yelled. I did, in a straight line.

He also ran for the car, taking a more zig-zag course. We

19

dragged the doors open, his fiancee fell in the back and he started the engine and headed in screaming first gear for the gates. Narrow gates, into which at that moment turned the car of the College President. With the awful courage of the plastered, my friend attempted to pass him on the inside, and stove in the side of his car.

I decided it was time I began to live a more peaceful and studious life. I had in fact planned to share a flat with a Jewish friend of mine, Michael Brennan, and we had spent several days following up classified ads. Eventually, we came upon a place in Drimnagh that looked perfect, and raced off with the first edition of the *Evening Mail* to see the landlady, who turned out to be a strange woman with a whispery manner of speech and a frantic compulsion to talk. We agreed to take the flat, and she, by way of return, gave us her entire life's history, which seemed to be as dramatic and tragedy-ridden as it was full of inconsistencies. I began to avoid Michael's eye, which was full of glee and which threatened to topple me into rude laughter.

"... so that's how I became a widow," she said, finishing one section of the saga. "And this is my dear husband, Lord Rest Him." She handed me a big glossy photograph. I gazed open-mouthed into the handsome face of Gregory Peck.

"Three years dead this spring," she whispered tearfully.

I must be wrong, I decided, and handed it to Michael. He gaped and reversed the print, handing it back to me with its back uppermost. PUBLICITY DEPARTMENT, MGM, it read. We managed to separate ourselves from Mr Peck's widow and get ourselves settled in, but the weirdness of the set up, coupled with the fact that she was only a thin partition away from us, sent us into helpless laughter. It was not helped by Michael's imitations of her, stroking the publicity still of the film star. He was in the middle of a spirited (if whispered) version of her monologue when she swung the door open and told the two of us to be off her premises in the morning. Michael later found somewhere else to stay, and I moved into a flat in Dufferin Avenue off the South Circular Road, and got down to more serious study.

But while the pre-clinical years spent studying Anatomy and

Physiology were very interesting, I cannot say that I really enjoyed medical school until the end of the third year, when we began to have some contact with the patients. Then it became real, and began to mean something. Just *what* it all meant, I was not sure. The first few weeks on the wards of the Richmond Hospital were among the most exciting of my life. Just to have a stethoscope of your own in your pocket was such a thrill — you'd walk down Grafton Street with it round your neck if you could. Not that there was any chance that you would become conceited. For one thing, there was a rigidly organised pecking order, and you were the last on it. *Everybody* could, and did, wipe their boots on students. And then there were my particular problems which, as always, stemmed from money, or the lack of it.

Around the time when we first went onto the wards, the pair of shoes I had began to die. They had holes everywhere and were too far gone for any repairer to do anything with them. It was absolutely imperative that I find some new footwear, but I had no money to spare. So I took a Saturday job at the Racing Board, for which I got 27/6d, and, just before the shops closed, I rushed around to buy a pair of shoes, only to find that whatever 27/6d would buy, it wouldn't stretch to a pair of shoes. Deflated, I bought a pair of sandals and some thick socks.

Those sandals caused me endless misery. They had a squeak that could be heard a mile away. Nothing could silence it. I rubbed grease into them. Friends doused them in oil, and bent them this way and that. Nothing worked. They squeaked on, inexorably, like a nightmare accompaniment to whatever I was doing. Of course, what I was doing involved a great deal of walking. Imagine it — the procession. In the lead the surgeon or consultant, accompanied by the Registrar and his housemen, flanked by nursing sisters, followed at a respectful distance by nurses, and trailed, even more respectfully, by the students. Last in line, squeak, squeak, squeak, John O'Connell.

The jokes were obvious and merciless. Some of the consultants only knew me as the one with the squeaky sandals, and the patients could tell it was me long before they saw me. Looking back, it's funny. At the time, it was pure misery, partly

21

because I was selfconscious at the best of times and each joke was a physical blow, but also because I knew students were expected to dress well, and it was a real fear that if I didn't lose my place because of failing an exam, I might lose it because of my 27/6d sandals.

Even in those early stages, I was fascinated by how docile the patients were. The consultant, on his rounds, virtually never spoke directly to the patient.

"What's wrong here?" he would ask the sister or another doctor. The patient lay there silently. Nurses ran around in advance, straightening beds and cleaning everybody up as if they were due for an army inspection. Then came our procession, with the students last, straining to hear what gems they could pick up. We lived in fear of almost everybody, but particularly of the sisters, who were queens in their own ward, and who tolerated students with only the bare minimum of courtesy, and sometimes with not even that. You might be sitting in your white coat beside a patient, who, perhaps, was not very clear as to whether you were a doctor or a student, when a sister would suddenly snatch away the screen and say "Take this screen down. No history-taking at teatime," or some other such remark.

It was all calculated to demean you and make you feel out of place. They did this even to qualified men. I remember once watching a surgeon do a most intricate and difficult heart operation — his finger was actually inside the chamber of the pulsating heart. After the operation I followed him when he went to a ward to seek a bed for a patient of his. The sister looked him up and down.

"You're only a Junior Surgeon," she said frozenly. "You're not entitled to any beds." It seemed to me very unjust that a man who had just saved a life and done a most marvellous operation, should be treated like a schoolboy, but it was the order of the day.

Not all operations were such a joy to watch. One of the first times I was ever in Theatre, I witnessed an operation which took some time, and all of the time, the anaesthetist read the *Irish Times*.

"How's she doing?" the surgeon would ask.

"Fine, fine," the anaesthetist would respond, blithely.

22

More time passed.

"Is she all right?" the surgeon asked, doubtfully.

"She's perfect," the anaesthetist snapped, still reading the paper.

Next thing the woman's heart stopped. The surgeon shouted, and the anaesthetist flung away the paper and went to work like a maniac trying to revive her, but it was too late.

"You bloody well killed her," yelled the surgeon. That was the last we students heard, for we were hastily ushered out of the theatre. I went back to where some of the others were having a meal, and told them the story. One of the older ones laughed.

"Don't worry about it. You were just unlucky on your first day."

It was nearly as bad the time I was doing the post mortem with another student and he was called away. At this time, in the Richmond Hospital a great many autopsies were done without the permission of relatives. Things have changed now. But then we waited until after midnight, and did the post mortem behind locked doors to deter prowlers who might ask inquisitive questions. One night, another student and I were working away on a dead person when there was a knock on the door. It was a nurse, looking for my co-worker for some reason. He went off, and I went on with what I was doing.

Not long after, another nurse arrived, this time looking for me, and I went to open the door, to discover that my friend had automatically locked it after him. Horror washed over me. I was locked in. The nurse went off to try to find him, and I concentrated on fighting the fear I have had of being locked in with the dead since my experience with my brother Sylvie's body. There were five corpses in the post mortem room, and two next door in the mortuary. Five sets of eyes watched me, from faces I had known up to hours before as living people. Cold sweat broke out on me, and I was afraid to turn my back on any one of them. I sang to keep my courage up until my friend came back with the key.

Generally speaking, I felt the dead were better off than the living when it came to accepting our interventions. As students, we seemed to be let loose on the public with painfully little practical training. It was a wonder to me that there weren't disasters. One of them nearly happened to me, when I had, unsupervised, to stitch a wound on a woman's face one inch south of her eye. I had the stitching almost completed when I realised I had no scissors.

"Get me a scalpel blade," I said to the student who was with me.

Scalpel blades were kept in a bath of Lysol - a very strong disinfectant. He lifted it out of the Lysol, and into my hand in one movement, without washing off the disinfectant. Of course, Lysol splashed near the woman's eye. We were lucky that she suffered no damage.

At the same time, the work was intensely rewarding. I never suffered nausea in the theatre, or boredom. I didn't know what a clock was, I loved the work so dearly. I loved the patients, too. I seemed to have a good rapport with them, and when someone I knew died I would talk about it and puzzle about it with other students, working out if we thought there was any way the patient might have been saved. We rarely criticised any of the senior men. They were Gods, omnipotent. It was only later, as interns, that we would comment unfavourably on a particular method of treatment. But at that time, they were too far above us.

We were in such awe of these consultants that I was rather nervous about approaching one to see if he would examine my mother, who by then had developed serious heart disease. He said he would, and he drove me to our small house, in Drumcondra. My mother was brought down to the parlour to be examined.

"For Chrissake," he said, "why can't I examine the woman in bed, where she should be?"

My mother's face tightened with anxiety, and I shook my head. Our parlour was respectable — more respectable than a sick person's bedroom could be kept — and you wanted to put the best side out.

One of the effects of working in hospitals for many years was to rob you of the sometimes exaggerated respect lay people tend to have for doctors. You see too many sides to their work, too many incidents which make you realise that they are skilled, but still human, still open to miscalculation. It was a miscalculation, rather than a mistake, that I remember causing one of the most horrifying things I ever saw in an operating theatre. The patient was a woman, the first wife of Dublin's famous comedian, Jimmy O'Dea, who had had a brain operation some years previously, as a result of which she had developed adhesions behind the eye, which were causing blindness. The surgeon had decided to remove the adhesions in an effort to preserve her sight, and to that end, had opened her skull, letting a door-like section of skull hang down in front of the eye while he operated. It was successful, and the patient was returned to the ward. Within minutes, however, there was bleeding at the site, and it was decided to take her back into the theatre and fix it. The surgeon reckoned that as she was still so deeply asleep there was no need to "top up" the anaesthetic, so he opened the skull, and began to cauterise where it was bleeding. And Mrs O'Dea woke up — to find a great lump of her skull hanging down over her eye, and someone cauterising inside it.

She screamed in terror, and then in pain every time he cauterised, but there was nothing he could do at that stage but reassure her as he continued cauterising. It is not the sort of thing you forget, either as surgeon, patient or student.

# Chapter 2

# Delivering Babies into Poverty

Most enjoyable of all during this period was maternity work. We spent a couple of months at Dublin's Coombe Hospital, where one of our duties as students was to take off on bicycles around the area to deliver babies in people's homes. Home births are at an all-time low in Ireland now, but at that time they were common. The system was that you went and delivered the baby, unless there were complications, in which case the hospital had an emergency squad that came out, or else they sent an ambulance and took the mother into the hospital.

Home deliveries may have had advantages — closeness of the rest of the family to what is a family event —but they also meant, in the majority of the cases I saw, that the mother was back at work, back looking after the other children within a few days, whereas in hospital, she might get a few days of enforced rest. In a lot of cases, what little the family had was shared between so many that even the normal provisions for a birth were not available. Sometimes, there was not even milk to provide the mother with a cup of tea when the birth was over.

Nevertheless, there was a powerful sense of satisfaction in this kind of work, despite the bad conditions. Your own living accommodation in the old Coombe Hospital consisted of what might be more appropriately termed horse boxes. Cubicles so small you had to go in sideways to get into your bed, with partitions four feet high separating one cubicle from the next — makeshift arrangements for the students in residence in the hospital.

The old Coombe Hospital was situated close to O'Keeffes the Knackers, a horse meat factory, with the result that the hospital was infested with flies. How basic hygiene was preserved there was a mystery. At lunch in the hospital canteen the students had to swoop on the food before the flies did. One postgraduate doctor from abroad left after two days in disgust at the lack of hygiene in the hospital.

We were worked so hard we were constantly exhausted. For that reason, it is fortunate that nature herself takes care of so many births. She would not want to have depended on us all the time. Certainly not the night I was on duty and four of us were involved in a game of cards. The game had reached a crucial stage when a call came for me to go to a woman who was in the throes of labour on the Crumlin Road.

"Bloody hell," one of the card players said. "Now what do we do?"

I put my coat on.

"We'll bloody well go with him," the same player said, inspired. "That's what we'll do." And they did, picking up the card game as soon as we arrived at the house.

Traditionally, what we did on arriving was to tell the woman to walk around, in order to bring on the contractions, and sit down ourselves, to get some rest. Occasionally, we'd get the woman walking and lie down on the bed for a quick nap before the real action started. But too often we were repelled by the masses of fleas that hopped about the bedclothes.

On this occasion we examined the woman, got her walking, and sat down at the table to continue the game of cards. She made muffled noises behind us, and one of us budding doctors would murmur consolingly.

"You'll be all right, Missus," we'd say. Or "You're doing grand."

Then, suddenly there was a different sound. A very distinctive sound.

Cry, as of baby.

Cards went flying, and the four student medics leaped to attention, only to find the woman had quietly gone on with the job herself, and the baby was now delivered. Behind our backs.

There were times, however, when we were of very real assistance, like the occasion when we were called to a woman whose own obstetrician couldn't be found. When we arrived, she was in a very bad way, because the birth had been precipitate. She was hanging on to the bed and the baby was already partly born in great distress.

We delivered the baby — my student friend Dayal Bhana and myself — and made the woman comfortable. Then we washed the baby and bedded it down. After that we made the woman tea and took it to her, and then, because she was so distressed about it, we cleaned up the room, washing the carpet. When we left, everything was in good order, with a perfect baby and a happy mother close to each other and comfortable.

We had, as part of the routine, to call again the next day, and when we knocked at the door, the woman's husband answered.

"Oh," he said, obviously taken aback. "Oh, it's you. Oh. Well, her Doctor is with her at the moment, so she can't be disturbed. Do we owe you anything?"

Her Doctor, who had not been around when she needed him, could not be disturbed. We were turned away like tradesmen touting for business.

The great satisfaction about medicine, however, is that things balance out. For every disappointment, there is a joy. For every family like that woman's, there is one where you are made to feel that this new baby is a major and happy event and that you are part of the family because of the part you have played in bringing the baby into it. Sometimes the family can be very forceful in their appreciation.

On duty as a student one night in the Coombe, I received an urgent call to deliver a woman at the Portobello Nursing Home. The call was for the Assistant Master whose patient was about to deliver. He not being available, I hurried to the nursing home and completed the delivery. The following day, when I went to make my routine follow-up call, the Assistant Master of the Coombe was there. I was nervous, but I carried out my examination under his watchful eye, and did so each morning. At the end of the week, the woman handed me a cheque. I immediately handed it to the Assistant Master, assuming that as she was his case he would therefore expect it.

"This is for you, Sir," I said.

The woman snatched it out of his hand.

"Oh, no it isn't," she said addressing me. "You delivered my baby. You get paid."

The Assistant master waved at it in a dismissive way, and I pocketed it in great delight.

Unfortunately, on the occasion when I got the most fervent gratitude, it was misplaced. The birth was a difficult and complicated Caesarian in the Coombe Hospital, and my only function was to stand, masked and gowned and sterile, beside the Obstetrician, to wipe his brow.

"Wipe," he would say, and I'd apply an absorbent pad to remove the sweat. In due course, the baby was delivered, the mother prepared for return to the ward, and we came out of the theatre to take off our caps and gowns.

On the way out, a white-faced young man, very obviously the father, was waiting. As I came out, first, he made a pass at stopping me.

"It's OK," I said, very conscious of the surgeon stumping behind me. "It's a boy and they're both fine."

"Oh, God, Oh, God, thank you, thank you," he said. "They told me you were a great surgeon, and they were right."

The surgeon, passing by, anonymous in his green outfit and mask, cast me a quizzical glance. The happy father burbled on.

"I'll remember this always to you," he said earnestly. "And we'll name the baby after you."

Out in the tenements, of course, there was nobody to wipe the forehead of the attending medic. Quite often, there were not even the basics of care. No towels, no sheets. Just newspapers. And even then, there were limitations. I remember dealing with one case where the mother of the woman about to give birth noticed me lifting the pile of newspapers to use.

"Hey, not that top one," she said."That's today's, and I haven't read it yet."

Hygiene was primitive. We brought the Dettol with us and cleaned as well as we could, but with people  living in overcrowded conditions, dirt was an ever-present unshiftable fact of life. In Georgian houses with beautiful exteriors you found whole families living in curtained off tiny sub-sections of a fourth floor room. The walls were covered in a uniform dark red powder pigment called "raddle," and you could not walk into one of these houses without leaving with raddle on the shoulders of your jacket.

For those who lived on the top floors, the water supply and the toilet were four flights of stairs down. Little wonder, then, that Dublin had a ghastly record of child death from gastro-enteritis. A feeding bottle would be dropped on the floor, retrieved and "cleaned" by a quick parental lick of the tongue before re-insertion in the toddler's mouth. Given what the floor was covered in, it was an unavoidable recipe for disaster. Parasites were everywhere. One of the strange things I learned was that when someone died, you did not even have to be close to the patient to know the moment of death; the lice would leave them like a grey moving carpet.

Families were big. I remember in the Coombe Out patients dealing as a matter of routine with mothers of ten children. On one occasion, I was examining a mother when she said to me "This is my eighteenth, and my daughter is in the next cubicle and it's her thirteenth." There was no family planning, and anything that suggested family planning provoked prejudice. Because of my own background, I was not immune to this prejudice myself.

The classic example of that was when I went out to take care of a woman who had just had a miscarriage. On the windowsill in her room I saw a condom. My immediate reaction was that the miscarriage served her right, because she had obviously been flying in the face of God (albeit not very successfully, since she had become pregnant). I was still a student and I still had a great deal to learn, not just about medicine, but about values and judgement and human rights.

It was at this time that the infamous Dublin abortionist, Nurse Caden, was operating. I knew one of the women who died at her hands. What happened was that I was in the habit of going into a coffee house where I met a man called Jack O'Reilly, who had achieved notoriety because he had been broadcasting for the Germans during the war and later a German plane had dropped him by parachute over Ireland and he made his way down to his father's house in Clare. His father was an old RIC man, and held strongly to a law-and-order philosophy. He promptly handed the son over to the authorities, who interned him at the Curragh. Eventually, he was released, and using the money (about £20,000) he had on him when he was dropped over Ireland, he bought the Esplanade Hotel, which was later to become the Ashling Hotel in Parkgate Street. Jack O'Reilly came into this coffee house regularly. So did his wife, with whom he was not living. If both were there at the same time, I drank my tea on my own. If he was there on his own, I joined him. If she was there on her own, I joined her.

She had worked as a maid in a house in Drumcondra when I was a child, and she often told me she remembered spotting me on my way to school while she was polishing the brass door knockers. Jack O'Reilly went off to live in South Africa and it appears his wife got pregnant by someone else. She evidently decided to have an abortion and went to Nurse Caden to have it done. When it went disastrously wrong, Nurse Caden decided that if the woman was going to die, she was certainly not going to be allowed to die on her premises, and got her mobile enough to push her out on the footpath in Hume Street, where she died a few feet away and was later found by a patient of mine.

The notorious Nurse Caden was later convicted, and the case horrified people, exposing the terror of unwed motherhood that would drive women to endanger their health and their lives. Nurse Caden was the highly publicised case where the abortionist got caught. There were others who did not get caught. One doctor, at that time, was known to do abortions. But he had an advanced sense of self-protection, so that at one stage when a middle-class businessman brought a girl to him and asked fairly bluntly for an abortion, the doctor quickly called the police and had the man taken to court on a charge of abortion-procuring. This doctor continued to do his discreet abortions for years, undiscovered by the law because none of the women who found their way to him died on his doorstep, as happened with Nurse Caden's patients.

31

The other tragedy of the time was diphtheria. Today, it's a minor problem to equip medical students with an understanding of diphtheria, because there are so few cases to be seen these days. Then, it was rife, causing the agonising death of so many children. Cork Street Fever Hospital was a famous hospital where diphtheria sufferers were taken. If you had one in your family, it was like a medieval plague. Your child was taken away from you, and you were never allowed to visit, because it was so easy to catch the illness. You were given a number, and each evening in the newspaper, you could check up on how that number was doing. That was the way parents learned that their child, or children, had died in Cork Street. The children died, were coffined immediately without the parents being permitted to see the bodies of their loved ones. The tiny coffins were commonly brought to the cemetery on the back of a bicycle.

One little girl was taken to Cork Street with diphtheria and duly became a number. Her parents invested in the newspaper every day, and one day learned the bad news. She was dead. As usual the parents never saw the body but arranged for her quick burial and then went on with their lives and tried to forget about their daughter.

Except that she had *not* died. The number went into the paper by mistake. The administration in the hospital had wrongly confused her name with that of an orphan from Limerick who did die. The mix-up meant that the young Dublin child was despatched to an orphanage in Limerick, where she grew up. In her late teens, the orphanage found her a job as a maid in Dublin, around the corner from where she had lived as a child and where her parents still lived. Even though she had been only a toddler when she was taken into Cork Street Fever Hospital, the location sparked memories. Things began to click together in her mind and she eventually found her family, sixteen years after she had been taken from them.

As a medical student, I heard tragic stories every day, but the daily tasks and the pressure of study made them seem inevitable, and prevented me noticing that they fitted into a pattern of poverty and deprivation that could be challenged. That realisation came later, with the arrival in my life of Dayal

Bhana.

In my fourth year at College, I went to live in a flat, on Elgin Road, Ballsbridge. Prosaically enough, it was a converted toilet, in a house where another flat was taken by an Indian named Dayal Bhana. Bhana had qualified as a lawyer at Edinburgh University, but then found that he didn't like law, and wanted to do medicine. He was a clever, cultured, generous person, and I was lucky to meet him when I did. Because of the amount of my time and energy absorbed by study, his views, and the fact that his philosophy of life was so far from my own, made relatively little impact on me. It is one of the comments often made about medical students, of course, that if they work at their studies, they have no time to be interested in literature or politics or anything else. I was aware, in a vague way, that Bhana thought differently from me on a number of issues, but he was not a proselytiser, and even if he had been, I was too preoccupied to make a good convert. Little indications got through to me. When I went to a party of his friends, a book on the bed attracted my attention - a fierce little tract against the Catholic Church. I read a bit.

"Do you read this?" I asked. There were nods. "It's interesting," I said, and forgot about it. When the Queen of England flew to Canada for a State visit, I found him reading the paper with the report in it.

"I'm an atheist, John. But I found myself saying a fervent prayer that her plane would come down in the drink, I hate British Royalty so much."

And there was the episode about the Korean War. We had an American post-graduate student in the Hospital, and one day, he and Bhana got into an argument. American and Indian went at it full blast, and we ignorant Irish gaped from side to side, like people watching a tennis match without knowing the rules. Bhana was for the North Koreans, which seemed to us to have little significance. It maddened the American.

"Why don't you climb back in the hole you crawled out of, you sewer rat of a Communist?" was one of his milder comments to Bhana.

Gradually, although he never proclaimed himself anything

33

in particular, I realised that Bhana was a Communist. Here was I, daily Mass-goer, becoming close pals with an atheist, and the strange thing about it was that it never cost me a thought. I put his beliefs in one mental box, and his character in another mental box, and never worried about juggling the two. As far as I was concerned, he was simply a good man and a good friend. In practical things, he conformed to that old cliché about a pal being the one to give you the shirt off his back. In Bhana's case, it was a coat.

The winter of 1953 was a particularly bitter one, and I was without an overcoat, so that two of us took turns with his overcoat, one of us staying in the flat while the other went to clinic. Even with the use of the coat, it was a lean time. I got flu, and piled newspapers on my bed to keep warm. This wasn't new to our family — newspapers are great insulators, and had been used in the past when blankets were scarce. Housekeeping was skimpy and you lived from day to day, buying two ounces of butter when you could, living on tea, bread and occasionally, minced meat.

Miraculously, apart from the bout of flu, I kept well, and, although I was still short of money, for the first time I began to have a sense that I was pulling on that lifeline, heading for somewhere. Unfortunately, that sensation made me less rather than more sensitive to the evidence of other people's misery. I snapped out a comment about some patient, evidently very poor, and Bhana very calmly pulled me up on it.

"It's not of his doing that he's in that position," he said. "You must not be trying to distance yourself from indigence."

That was one of his idiosyncrasies. He played with the English language as a chess master plays chess — always going for the strange and inventive, rather than the happily workaday phrase. Where I would say "Take your feet off the table, you're wrecking it," Bhana would say, "Kindly remove your extremities from the table, you will be dislocating it."

He was also one of the most meticulous and hardworking students I had met, although he never had the luck he deserved. There was one night on duty as a student in Mercer's hospital that he swapped with me because he wanted to go to a dance,

34

and, when he came back in he took over from me. Not long after he came back, there was a call for him to go down to Casualty, and when he got there, an elderly man some Gardai had brought in was there, drunk, having fallen about all over the place. Bhana carried out the most detailed examination, wrote up all his notes, made the man comfortable, and went back to bed, sleeping late the next morning. I went down in the late morning to find a group of visitors clustered around the cot in the casualty ward — the man was dead. Brain haemorrhage. Bhana got it in the neck because he had not called the house surgeon. The problem, from our point of view as students, was that you were always unwilling to call the house surgeons because they made it clear they did not want to be bothered unless the sky was falling.

As if this was not bad enough, a second incident followed within a short time. On this occasion, a man was brought in, having been knocked off his bike in the city centre, and, again, Bhana did a complete check, under some pressure, because the man was making a fuss.

"Look," he kept saying, "I'm a busy man. And my company isn't going to pay me for while I'm in here. And I only fell off the bloody bicycle, I mean, I wasn't trampled underfoot or anything, so will you do us a favour, will you? Will you just stop messing around and let me get back to work? This is costing me money, you know."

Eventually, Bhana let him go. Later that night, he was admitted to another hospital with a fractured skull, the word was returned to our Senior Surgeon, and Bhana was in deep and extremely hot water over a technicality.

The point which was made repeatedly was not that Bhana had made a mistake in letting the man go, but that he had made a mistake in not getting the man to sign himself out — a self-protective mechanism by which hospitals avoided expensive litigation after the event. His fault, then, was not so much a medical fault as a political fault. He was severely reprimanded, although the reprimand was somewhat mitigated by the Senior Physician's comment that he was an exemplary student and it was "just one of those things". He was shaken to the roots of his being, not only because he held himself responsible, but because he felt he had in some way failed in his mission in life, which was to serve people.

While we shared adjoining flats, he taught me to love classical music, which is still a constant pleasure and means of relaxation. Each night at about ten thirty, I would go to his flat, and for three quarters of an hour, he would play records, often of ballet music Once, we even went to the Ballet. He had the tickets, and for me, it was a new and magical experience.

Most of our time as students, however, was spent in finding and following the best hospital clinicians — those consultants who had a reputation for explaining and making clear whatever illness it was they were describing. Not that it was easy to pick your clinician. You looked for the best guy, of course, but there was a politicking element to it, too.

You had to make sure to get to your examiner's clinics, because although they pretended to be above noticing who was there and who wasn't, it was known that they could list the names of participants after each session. In addition, you had to spot each examiner's peculiarities, and the way he liked answers framed.

Some of the consultants were fascinating to watch. I remember one great big man in Baggot Street Hospital, Surgeon Jack Henry, who should have been an Abbey actor, and whose progress through a ward was witnessed by as many open mouths as there were people there. He had a massive personality and a great swooping voice, and his gestures were wide, generous and calculated. I particularly remember how he related the incident of the patient with the full and obstructed bladder — the prize story in his repertoire.

"I was called to the house of an unfortunate fellow, who was in agony because he couldn't urinate. I was therefore compelled to insert a catheter into his bladder to relieve his distress. Can you imagine my dismay when, within seconds, he expired before my very eyes." A long sorrowful pause. "The tragedy, gentlemen, was not that the patient died but that my cheque lay unsigned on his mantlepiece." Said, no doubt, for effect. This man did not so much comment on a patient's

36

condition — he orated. Like many of the other consultants, he was never known to refer to patients as people. They were The Liver. Or This Heart. Or The Kidneys. Even at the time, I thought this attention to individual organs was crazy. The notion that you could cure a man just by looking at or listening to a diseased heart, made no sense to me. I felt there should have been much more attention to the whole person, their lifestyle, attitudes, way of behaving — a holistic approach — which in fact has since become more fashionable.

As students, we followed in large groups, often as many as sixty at a time, in the wake of a consultant surgeon or physician, and it was agony to be picked out from that comfortingly anonymous group and asked to examine a patient, especially if you made a mistake. One whopper I once made was to miss an alcoholic's large liver. It was pointed out by Professor Paddy McNally and I waited for the ceiling to arrive around my ears. Instead he smiled with unexpected gentleness, and said "I'll guarantee you won't make that mistake again, will you?" Of course I never did.

And many a student was castigated for his lack of observation. "Before the advent of these new fangled tests for detecting sugar in the urine," said one consultant whose speciality was diabetes, "a clinician of old would dip his finger into the urine specimen and taste it for sugar, just as I am doing now." At that he inserted a finger in the specimen of urine and then put a finger to his lips.

"Now gentlemen," he said to the students, "let me see you do likewise." At which every student dipped his finger into the urine and then put the finger in his mouth.

At that point, the Consultant bawled, "What fools you all are with no powers of observation. Had you been observing me closely you would have seen that I put my index finger in the urine, but I put my middle finger to my lips." The patients in the beds howled with laughter when they saw the foolish expressions on the faces of the students.

Patients at that time seemed quite happy to have congregations of students surveying their charts and their bodies. Now, when people are more educated about their rights,

I suspect that this willingness to be the subject of a lecture has decreased, but then there was a kind of morbid desire to see what "this lot will make of me", and of course, it did make lonely, tired and sick people the centre of attention, for however short a time.

Coming up to my Finals, I had regained a little of the confidence my father had always given us. I was sure of getting through. What I wanted to do was not merely get through, but to win the coveted Council prize which would have meant a gold medal (honour and glory) and £100 (real live money.) In the event, I only got two of the three honours required and always felt cross that I had not got the third.

Graduation day. The high point in a student's life, when, gowned and neatly suited, he approaches the rostrum. Neatly suited? My suit was in tatters. So I borrowed a suit from a five foot eight friend. I am five foot six and a half. It fell in concertina folds around my ankles. Never mind, I thought, no more obstacles. Well, yes, someone said. There IS the fifty pounds. WHAT fifty pounds? I yelled in terror. I hadn't fifty pence, never mind fifty pounds. Yes, the knowing one explained. Fifty pounds graduation fee. If you did not have it, no graduation. It had to be lodged to the bank account of the College before twelve o'clock. It was now ten. I sat down in total despair. Everything I had worked for was about to be snatched away because of my lack of this arbitrary fifty pounds. My Indian friend Bhana said he would do his best, but he hadn't fifty pounds to spare. He disappeared and I sat, slumped in total misery.

"The situation is somewhat more advantageous than at first blush," he announced, returning an hour later. In his hand, fifty pound notes. He had gone, barracked all of his friends and acquaintances on my behalf, and finally managed to borrow it from, I believe, Dominic Behan who did not know John O'Connell, and to this day probably has no idea of the gratitude of the student with the concertina folds of cloth around his ankles. We raced to the bank, deposited it, graduated at 12 noon. Graduation was a memorable occasion for me as my mother and my sister Pam attended the ceremony. My father in

38

his usual retiring way preferred to stay at home but was very proud of the photographs taken at the ceremony. At two o'clock I checked in as an intern in Mercer's. Bhana went to Dr Steeven's Hospital and thence to London, where I was able to return the favour he had done me on graduation day to some small extent by tiding him over a bad financial period.

My first day in Mercer's Hospital as an intern might well have been my last, over the incident of the broken finger. A patient came in that evening with a broken finger, and the Sister in charge insisted that the patient go home and return the following day, to be dealt with by Casualty. I thought that this was silly, and said so, using a line of thinking which was to cause me trouble then and later in my political career. The line of thinking runs thus — Here is a problem. (In this case, one broken finger.) There is a solution. (In this case, my skills and the hospital's equipment.) Put the two together, and we can all go home to our beds happy that a good day's work has been done. Unfortunately, there are always people around who are quite happy to see problems on one side, and solutions on the other, unlikely to meet until you "go through the proper channels". In my experience, the "proper channels," are circuitous and wasteful time-absorbers put in the way of action by lazy or frightened or bureaucratic people who forget about real people and their real problems.

So here we were, this broken finger, its owner, and me. The sister was adamant, but so was I, and if there was a competition in determination, I would back myself against all comers. I fixed the finger. The sister promptly fixed me. She reported me to the Senior Surgeon, a Mr Bouchier Hayes. I was called to his office, and went with, if not a singing heart, at least with a small element of confidence that this man would support me, since it was said that he had been expelled from another hospital some time in his earlier surgical career after a confrontation with a sister.

I was to be proved wrong. He listened to my side of the story, nodded wearily and then fixed me with sad, resigned eyes.

"O'Connell," he began, and sighed. "O'Connell, we must be

realistic. It is easier to get house surgeons than it is to get sisters."

So I had to allow the sister to boss me around. It would be satisfyingly dramatic if I could tell of having had a clever and subtle revenge on her, but in fact we grew to be great friends, and she ended up as a patient of mine.

From that year on, I saw little of Bhana, as I am not good at maintaining long distance relationships, although I never lose the great attachment I form to a few friends. When he was killed some years ago in a road accident in Canada, I was greatly grieved. Later, I was approached to see if I could help his daughter, brought up in this country and now eager to study medicine, but unsuccessful in getting into the College of Surgeons. I phoned the Dean there, Dr Harry O'Flanagan, and reminded him of Bhana's brilliance, hard work and great personal charm. Bhana's daughter was subsequently accepted, and I was relieved that I could repay part of the life-debt I owed him. In many ways, it was he who re-sensitised me to what poverty meant, at a time when I would have been all too happy to climb away from it and reject it, and so, indirectly, he put me into politics. Indirectly, and a little later. More immediately came my internship.

My intern year was perhaps the most exciting year of my life. After six years of relative obscurity, the "doctor" title had catapulted me into a position of responsibility. A new status. Ward sisters who a short time previously had treated me with total scorn were now seeking my advice.

"Dr O'Connell, would you please advise treatment for that new admission?"

"Dr O'Connell, we need you in casualty!"

"Dr O'Connell, could Mrs So and So be discharged?"

Bewildering, frightening. An overpowering urge to rush to the textbooks for guidance. This won't do, I say to myself. I must make the decisions. After a little trepidation, I found myself scrawling instructions on the patient's charts, ordering a blood transfusion for the casualty case, and saying, "It's OK for Mrs So-and-So to go home, she's fit and well." Gradually the confidence grows and even the consultants give grudging recognition.

My intern year flew, and what I vividly remember of it is that there was a constant struggle to manage without meat, since I had given up all forms of meat six months before my Finals, as a sacrifice to ensure success. Today, people don't do that sort of thing, but then it was normal, although not normal enough for the hospital to provide vegetarian meals without a fuss. Luckily, a senior physician, Dr Joe Lewis, also turned out to be a vegetarian, and he made it clear that I was to stick to my guns until the kitchen sister eventually gave in.

At the end of the year, I decided that I was going to America for a few years, and the hospital over there sent my plane ticket. First, it was marriage to Lillian, whom I'd been keeping company with for a few years, and then it was off to America. We had swapped the plane ticket for two sailing tickets, and the trip was six days of hell. I was dreadfully sick, and my Lillian found herself playing nurse after ten days of marriage, caring for someone who had epic seasickness complicated by vaccination reaction. I was still so ill when I arrived in New York that I decided I should visit a hospital and seek treatment.

I remember one man who was admitted to Mercer's Hospital with a broken leg, whom the almoner (now known as the medical social worker) pursued up to the ward to interview about his financial circumstances. "You can't stay here, you know, without paying," she informed him in a ringing soprano. "You can't stay here if you can't cover yourself financially."

The man with the broken leg looked at her with pure hatred.

"Then get an ambulance," he said. "Because I wouldn't stay in this bloody dump if I was being PAID, never mind paying."

There was the usual flutter of well-meaning softening remarks from other people. Oh, she didn't really mean it. Oh, if his circumstances weren't the best, they could probably come to some sort of ... Oh, relax for the moment, there's no need to take it like that.

"Get an ambulance," the man insisted. "I'm going home."

And home he went. With that in mind, I waited in the American hospital for attention and was duly accosted.

"Twenty dollars, please," the functionary said briskly.

41

"Twenty dollars?"

"Yeah. Twenty dollars."

"I'm afraid you must have the wrong person. I haven't been treated yet."

"No. And you won't be treated unless you've got twenty dollars."

I produced my twenty dollars and sat back to wait. Maybe there was something to be said about Irish almoners after all.

Indeed, those first weeks in the States were anything but pleasant. I was to work in a hospital run by the Sisters of Mercy, but when we arrived in Ohio, I found that renting an apartment used up every last penny I had. Next morning I had to report at 7.30 for work, breakfastless and nervous. The Chief of Medical Staff saw me in his office over a cup of coffee. And when I say "over", that's what I mean. We discussed what I would do while he drank the coffee. I was ravenously hungry and desperately thirsty, but I was too timid to ask him for coffee, and it never occurred to him to offer it.

The food was different. The hospital routine was different. And the heat was horrendous. Peripherals can be adapted to. You remark upon the food, but it doesn't change you, doesn't confuse your mind. Attitudes, ways of seeing things are more difficult. The Mother Superior, Sister Mary Aquin, was a nun from Tralee. American Big Business in a habit and with a ruined Kerry accent. Calm, ruthless eyes on the patient. Heart. Very bad. Worse. Very poor.

"Get him out."

"Sorry?"

Face bland, confident that I had heard her the first time.

"But he'll die Sister!"

Expressionless.

"He'll die anyway, Doctor, Get him out."

Time and space taking on a new shape.

"Come to our party," from a group of interns.

Address? A number in the High Street. The Hospital is in the High Street. I set out to walk at seven at night and arrived at eleven, weak from heat and exhaustion, not realising that High Street extended for miles.

Poverty and prosperity took different shape in America than in Dublin. The migrant workers at the hospital's free clinic were despised and became my "property" once I evinced an interest. Later, they would pass me in their Chevys and Cadillacs as I walked, they thought, for my health. The poor had big cars and I, lonely, confused, shamed by the oddness of walking in a motorised country, could only compare what could be compared to Dublin's advantage. There were broken pavements.

Kicking loose stones, I mutter to myself.

"Wouldn't be tolerated in Dublin."

But there was learning too. An approach to medicine concerned with the whole patient, and a new attitude to life, summed up by the "sir" incidents.

In the beginning, I "Sirred" everybody, as we had been trained to do in Dublin. In the sitting-room of the hospital, when a white coat entered, I would bob up and sir. Half the time, as I soon discovered, I was sirring interns, who were some steps below me on the seniority ladder. Later, I learned to stop the courtesy entirely. What happened was that the American Chief of Staff suddenly asked me for an explanation of something that had happened.

"Well, Sir -" I began.

"Look," he said, "You don't 'sir' anybody here. Not anybody. OK?" "OK". I then told him about the consultant in Mercer's in Dublin.

"You met him at the door," I said. "And you greeted him by saying "Good morning, Sir," as you took his coat.

"Like a lackey?"

"Well, yes, I suppose so, but it was the way things were."

"I'd have given him a kick in the ass for himself," he replied.

The comment stayed with me and gestated.

Years later, back in Dublin, my first day on duty in the Mater Hospital, the consultant arrived and handed me his medical bag. I ignored it, and like an object in a cartoon, it seemed to hang there for a minute before crashing down and smashing its delicate instruments.

"If there is one thing America taught me," I told him,

43

stepping over the bag, "it is to be no man's lackey."

America also taught me to think differently about having worked my way through College. Everybody there had done precisely that, so that it was ordinary, expected. Where you came from mattered little. They cared only about achievement.

Debbie, our daughter, was born on 20 April 1956 — something of a celebrity at birth because she was born of Catholic parents in a nuns' hospital where everyone else was either Protestant or Mormon. At the moment of arrival, she was snatched from the obstetrician for Baptism by one of the nuns, assisted by another. Pouring water. Prayers. And the obstetrician who gazed in disgust.

"I thought we were trying to save the baby," he said, "not trying to drown it!"

A lovely, easy-going child, Debbie. Stricken with whooping cough at three months. Looking back, I was a mixture as a father, loving children, doing all the "female" things like changing and feeding, worrying a great deal about everything, and, after the baby stage, probably authoritarian.

That time in America passed in a spin of work and study intermingled with bouts of recurrent homesickness. A few incidents stay fresh. That first day, for instance. It started with the consultant taking me around corridors jammed with beds. There was a polio epidemic. Nurses laid warm cloths on the twisted muscles of the sufferers, and I was led to the bed of one — a twenty year old flanked by drawn-faced parents.

"You needn't worry," the consultant boomed confidently at them. "This is Dr O'Connell, fresh from Dublin and he'll be in charge of your son's case. If its necessary, he'll do a tracheotomy (an emergency operation on the windpipe to allow the patient to breathe). So you can feel very happy." I smiled through clenched teeth at the trio. Up to that morning, I had never seen a polio case, nor done a tracheotomy. Luckily for the young man (and me) he didn't need one.

I was brought into another room in the hospital to meet patient Eddie. The name is burned into my consciousness.

"Meet Eddie," the consultant said, his voice full of cheer and a little pride. "Eddie's been with us for three weeks — came in

44

with a severe coronary, and he's going home today. This is Dr. O'Connell from Ireland". I extended my hand. Eddie sat upright, shook it and fell back — stone dead. The consultant went into frenzied action, but nothing worked. Eddie was gone. I was known for several days as the doctor with the deadly handshake.

But then, on the other side, I was seeing some things which made ME somewhat less than totally confident in the hospital's senior staff. I was on the medical ward one day when a patient was brought in from the operating theatre, followed by the surgeon, beside himself with anxiety and rage. The woman had been admitted for a gall bladder operation.

"It wasn't a damn gall bladder," the surgeon fumed. "It was a coronary she had. Quick, put up an intravenous drip on her with Aramine to raise her blood pressure."

The blood pressure was critically low. I regulated the drip to allow a few drops a minute into the woman's vein, observing normal procedure. The surgeon promptly blew his top, snatched the little control from me and adjusted it so that Aramine was running into the vein at full speed.

"Running Aramine into the vein at that rate — she'll be dead," I protested.

"She'll be dead if you don't," he said, pushing me aside. Within the hour, the woman had died.

In Dublin, I had helped babies to be born into poverty, disease and deprivation of all kinds. In American, I had a glimpse of a sordid side of American life. Lima State Hospital for the Criminally Insane was located in the same town as my hospital and I was expected to provide medical cover for that institution. Appalled at the conditions but fascinated by the inmates, I was forever asking questions.

"Leroy, what brought you in here?"

"Killed my girlfriend." Spoken as if he was describing the cereal he'd had for breakfast.

"Why?"

"Cause I caught her with another man." Simple as that.

These were young, healthy men in a state mental institution because some persuasive lawyer convinced them that a plea of insanity with its consequent term in Lima Hospital for the Criminally Insane was better than risking the gas chamber or the electric chair. Men cooped up, lonely and depressed. I used to watch them through the window of the infirmary as they were herded out into the yard for their recreational period. Lifeless bundles of humanity, marching endlessly round an enclosed yard. Little wonder, I thought, the abnormally high suicide rate I witnessed among them. Without hope of remission all they had to look forward to was a lifetime in a mental institution. Hanging oneself from the ceiling of the cell was a crude, but effective, way out. It was often availed of.

A few other incidents stay fresh. The nun who insisted that the ECG machine should not be used at night to determine whether or not a patient had had a heart-attack, and my vain fight with her. The surgeon doing so many D & C (dilation and curettage) operations on young girls for painful periods, so ably assisted by the nuns, and the subsequent court case which revealed that, with the nuns' innocent co-operation he had been carrying out regular abortions on the young girls.

In America, the stethoscope is a symbol of big business. The motto "profit before patients" could sum up so many of the incidents I observed in my three-year stint in the U.S. Polio patients were left out in the corridors while precious hospital wards were  converted to private suites for the wealthy. Americans on moderate incomes lived in mortal fear of the cost of medical care. I was bewildered when confronted by a middle-aged man who explained that he couldn't afford the necessary operation because he still hadn't paid off the hospital and funeral bills of his wife who had died during the Depression. I realised doctors were the highest social class in America. Fee-splitting, referrals, lucrative "elective" operations were the means used to achieve wealth and status.

As regards politics, for all of this time, I was as ignorant as a budgie. At home, politics was never mentioned. The great figures of the day were names in children's games — "in comes de Valera at the doorio" and no more. My father once saw Jim Larkin talking on the docks. It was told with the same uninterested observation he would have used had he seen a giraffe being unloaded for the Zoo. It had no meaning in our lives. Later, I found medicine a totally encompassing life. It absorbs all your brain, your speculation, your reading-time, your concern with people. Once or twice, I became aware of American politics, aware, for example, that the senior doctors, to a man, voted Republican. It gave me a sneaking liking for the Democrats, but no more.

At this time, too, I was gradually working to the position where, as people say, "a doctor can't be shocked". Still shockable when I went to America, I was taken aback by the level of VD among the poor, the blacks, and grieved when one thirteen year old girl showed unmistakable signs of the disease. I thought it was terrible.

Then it was over, and we packed and came home with our first child Debbie. Home, to Dublin, 1958, and the Mater. Dr John O'Connell, Registrar, Mater Hospital. Salary £9 a week, or £450 a year, depending on which way you looked at it, and whichever way you looked at it, it wasn't much. The flat ate up £4.50 of it every week. When I found that I was finished most evenings by six o'clock, I decided to put up a plate and go into private practice at night. It would help to make the money go further and it would give me more experience of real street medicine. Hospital medicine was grand, lovely, stimulating, but I couldn't see myself holding on for years with little or no prospect. I saw the job of registrar as a stepping stone. In the meantime, I borrowed two rooms on the South Circular Road from a family I knew, the Reddys, put up a plate, and waited with bated breath.

It was summer, and I would sit where I could see passers-by halt and examine the plate, and I would wonder if any of them would ever come in. And then it began to happen. Friends came along. People I treated in a clinic in the Mater Hospital came. They told other people. The Asian flu arrived, prostrating more people and creating the need for more doctors. A local Jewish doctor, Dr Manne Berber, phoned me, wished me luck and told me that there were so many patients in the area, that he and his two Jewish friends would happily refer them to me, and this they duly did. Two Christian doctors in the

47

locality objected to my arrival as they feared competition.

For a time, I ran my job in the Mater Hospital and my private practice side by side, efficiently enough. I made some changes in the Mater, remembering the long, miserable hours I had sat in queues there as a youngster. It made no sense for people to wait for hours until the consultant could see them in order for a routine examination to be carried out, so I ensured that the investigation went on before the consultant got to them. The result was that what had been a harrowing session lasting from ten in the morning until three in the afternoon was now finished by eleven. I felt this was important. Busy patients could get on with their work sooner, the fearful had less time to be sitting, stewing in their own apprehension, and the morbidly curious had fewer moments in which to probe or gloat.

Eventually, though, the jobs I held in tandem began to drain all my energies. Even sleeping for about five and a half hours a night, which has always been adequate for me, I was exhausted, so I gave up the job in the Mater Hospital and became a full time GP. The medical practice grew and grew, and I loved the work, cheerfully ignoring the advice of one of my medical friends, who had told me it was a bad idea to become familiar with my patients.

"Never make a friend a patient, or a patient of a friend," he said sagely.

What nonsense it turned out to be. On calls, I would be offered, and would take, cups of tea, be filled in on the backgrounds of people, learn about occupations and hobbies. It was better medicine, not worse that I dished out as a result. The two rooms I had borrowed couldn't be mine forever, though. The Reddy family who had lent them needed them, and at times they must have felt that the O'Connell medical machine was taking over, especially when Liam Reddy, who worked in a car assembly plant, was occasionally bundled into a white coat and pressed into service as a receptionist, black hands and all!. Then I saw a house for sale, and fell in love with it. It was on the South Circular Road. I phoned the auctioneer that night, named the house and explained why I was interested. The problem, I suggested, might be ready money.

"How much do you have saved?" he asked bluntly.

"Fifty pounds."

"Don't be mad! And for God's sake don't make a fool of yourself by bidding tomorrow. You'd need £400 for the deposit alone."

I went to the action nevertheless. Not to bid, but to watch the bids being made. One after another. One here, another there, and then the hammer fell.

"Sold to Dr O'Connell for £1,400."

Weak with shock, never having bid at all, I approached the auctioneer.

"Make out a post-dated cheque for £400 and get the hell out of here fast, you have four weeks to get the money," he said.

A building society lent me nine hundred pounds, and I went to a Jewish solicitor Max Abrahamson, recommended by my auctioneer, to sort out the details of the sale, and found that there was an extra hundred pounds involved for stamp duty, or something like that. Max Abrahamson was related to Dr Manne Berber who had telephoned to wish me good luck when I put up my plate, and very kindly lent me the money. Throwing my own fifty pounds into the kitty meant I still had to find four hundred and fifty within three weeks, so I took the begging bowl to friends.

"That's an awful house," one said. "Not suitable for a practice at all. I couldn't lend you money on that, you'd regret it."

"Are you mad?" another asked. "Sure that bloody place is on the wrong side of the road."

No luck anywhere as the days slipped past. There were two days to the deadline, and I was so worried I could scarcely concentrate on my work. On the evening of the second last day, one of my patients was a stranger, with a few drinks on him, in for a check-up.

"What's your occupation?" I asked, filling in my profile on him.

"You might say I'm a clerk," he said vaguely.

"Where?"

"In a bank."

49

"Oh. Oh. Hey, what's a bank's attitude to loans at the moment?"

"Hostile. There's a depression on, hadn't you noticed? Why?"

I hesitated. Should I tell him. Then I disclosed my problem.

"'Well, look, come down to the bank tomorrow and I'll see if there's anything I can do."

He gave me his name, and I said I'd be there next morning, only half hopeful, because you don't pin all your hopes on a man with a few drinks in him. Nevertheless, I went to the bank next day, the last day before the cheque had to be made good, and gave his name to a cashier. Did that man work there?

"Oh, yes, he's the manager. And you are?"

"John O'Connell. Dr John O'Connell."

"Oh, yes, Dr. O'Connell, he's expecting you."

He advanced all the money I needed, and we were able to move into the house. The sittingroom was to be the surgery, the diningroom the waiting room and the O'Connell stamping ground was the kitchen. For something like four years, we lived and I worked there, and we were there when the second of our five children, John, arrived,

It was from this base that I became aware, from quite a different angle, of the poverty that festers in Dublin, and of the unemployment that ate away at the morale of generation after generation. You might go to a house where, say, the man was sick.

"What does he work at?"

"He hasn't worked in years."

"Well, what DID he do?"

"Well, he hasn't worked for so long ..."

Because men didn't work, there was the constant problem of how they could pay for the prescriptions. It was the first, the inevitable question.

"How much will this cost?" They flapped it in their hands, suspiciously. If they had two children sick, they tried to stretch a prescription between them, because the money was so short.

Such widespread unemployment, affecting every family I visited, was a sad shock after being in America, where there was no shortage of jobs, where people expected to be able to move and to take up jobs wherever they moved to. Then there was the overcrowding, so that when you went on night calls, you saw rooms full of sleeping adults of both sexes. You interrupted meals of bread and tea; you were always conscious of the dirt. One house had a large hole in the middle of the cement floor, constantly full of dirty water, and we stepped over it on each visit.

The dispensary system O'Casey wrote about in *Hall of Healing* had not been changed into anything dignified or caring. The combination of that dispensary system and overworked doctors meant that people were treated with speed and brusqueness. This damaged enormously the self-esteem of the poor and unemployed. Many patients did not even know about the dispensary system; they had poor knowledge about their rights. When I went to attend to a sick baby in the middle of the night, I had to climb over the bodies of other sleepers, only to find the baby sleeping on bare springs — there were no mattresses, no bedclothes. Yet in all houses, an effort was made to provide the necessities for the doctor's visit — the bowl of water, towel and soap. This effort, against the awful background of poverty, was infinitely pathetic.

A deep concern began to build up in me. Something, I felt, had to be done. Something. By someone. Like who? Try the Archbishop. I wrote him a letter about poverty and unemployment, outlining the deprivation I saw and making suggestions. I believed that something could be done if every school, every church, every factory took on an extra worker as a gesture towards the poor. I said it was dreadful that people were left to deteriorate and lose their will to work for ever, and I asked him to make a public plea. In due course, a letter came in answer to mine. Dr Mc Quaid did not feel the problems I outlined were his concern. I wrote to him about the housing problem, because I was concerned about the possibility of incest in such crowded conditions. A response. Even more curt and more precisely defining this problem as being outside the Archbishop's concern.

It never occurred to me at this time to think in terms of

political solutions to problems. I always assumed that the Church had major responsibilities and that once alerted to the existence of problems, particularly problems with moral implications, it would move mountains to deal with those problems. I found it difficult to come to terms with its unwillingness to register the number and intensity of the problems I was seeing or to respond to them.

I felt more helpless than ever. But what could I do? I could tell poor patients that the last few visits after an illness were "purely social", and refuse payment, and I could fight a few battles, which I did with a growing anger. There was a battle, for instance, with the Dublin Health Authority when I began to poke holes in the dispensary system I have already mentioned. That system depended on a part-time doctor seeing hundreds of patients for split seconds and making out a prescription, which was then filled in the dispensary without charge.

I sent poor patients who didn't want the dispensary doctor, but who had to have their prescriptions filled at the dispensary, and they were turned away. I sent them again. Refused. At that point, I sent the Health Authority a registered letter saying that if they continued to refuse to make out medicines for my patients on my prescriptions, I would take them to court. They gave in.

It was the first of many battles, many situations in which I find myself talking vehemently, angrily, and in which someone says in a huffy voice, "Well, there's no need to shout, you know." I'm never conscious of raising my voice, but I get very angry. Particularly with bodies like Dublin Corporation, which seem to run to a set of inhuman internal rules which have nothing to do with the needs and problems of real, suffering people. I can remember when I was growing up, we lived in fear of Dublin Corporation, and once or twice, when money was scarce, my mother went to money lenders rather than fall behind in her rent payments. Dublin Corporation has always seemed to me to be almost deliberately cruel in its operations, watching and pursuing people like the Gestapo. All those phone calls.

Me: "But he's unemployed. He hasn't got a job."

52

Dublin Corporation: "Our information says he has."

Me: "Then get the Gardai, take him to court for fraud, but don't just use your suspicions against people to deprive them of their rights."

Often, I felt, Dublin Corporation ended up making criminals out of incompetent or poor people by its ludicrous all-or-nothing system. If someone fell into arrears with rent one week then they had to pay double rent the following week. A portion wouldn't do.

If you were two weeks in arrears, and you brought three quarters of the money, they wouldn't take it, so the person offering the cash went home and naturally spent it. In no time at all, a minor problem grew into something much more serious. Officialdom, represented for me by Dublin Corporation, has always been negative and heartless, never listening to people's problems, never understanding their circumstances, never informing them of their entitlements, playing a kind of cruel cat and mouse game with them instead of helping them to realise whatever potential they have. I may be slightly paranoid about Dublin Corporation, but it seems to me that if there is anybody there who cares about people, they have never had much influence. Even in small matters, no attention is paid to personal convenience. I remember visiting a four storey block of flats, and at the bottom of the stairs, was there a sign to say which flats were upstairs? No. On a medical call in the middle of the night, I might have to climb four sets of stairs in search of number 124, and find that this particular flat block only went as far as 123, and I had to go back down and start again — simply because whoever was responsible for those flats never gave an empathic thought to what it must be like for a real person living in them. Another example was the system whereby if a wife got into arrears, her husband had to be brought in and told, which often complicated the problem and left the woman with no dignity whatever.

However, even though I felt a growing anger at the way some of my patients had to live, I was working flat out all of the time. My partner, Dr Louis Regan and I were quite simply worked off our feet, so that the occasional night call which wasn't really necessary particularly infuriated him.

"God, I could choke them, getting me out of bed at four in the morning," he told me one evening. "And half the time I bawl out the first person I meet in the house. Then I go upstairs and some poor eejit's deadly sick and I'm all remorse."

"The trick," I told him, "Is to say nothing until you've seen the sick person. Then you're wide awake, and they're usually needing help, so you don't feel mad."

I felt mad one night though. Middle of the night, frantic call. Baby sick. Very sick. Come quick, please. Clothes thrown on, out into the night, drove to the house. Knock knock on the door. A voice from inside.

"Is that the doctor?"

"Yes."

"Well, it's all right now, the baby's gone to sleep and I don't want her disturbed. Goodnight."

My mother died at this time. She had suffered a stroke, but it was a virus pneumonia which had finally brought about her demise. She had been staying with me and I can remember in desperation trying to pump antibiotics into her, when someone called to my house to have me visit his wife.

"I'm sorry," I said. "I cannot go now, my own mother is quite ill."

"So is my wife," he shouted angrily, "and you're her doctor".

"OK" I said. "I'll call up to see your wife shortly."

When I did arrive at the patient's house she had a slight cold but was not confined to bed. It was more convenient for her to call me, than to have to travel down to my surgery. When I rushed home to see how my mother was, she was dead. I was full of remorse for a very long time.

My father died three years later. He was very proud of the fact that he had lived to see me become a doctor. In the end he developed leukaemia, and I had him admitted to St Laurence's Hospital, North Brunswick Street. He used to speak with fond memories of North Brunswick Street, having been born there, and on his daily walks around that area he actually used to kiss the spot where he and my mother had first met.

54

Now as he lay in the hospital ward in considerable discomfort from breathlessness and the pain of nurses sticking needles in his veins, he was clearly unhappy that I had put him in hospital.

"Offer it up," I said reassuringly, remembering those self same words he had so often uttered whenever any of us in the family suffered pain or tribulation.

"It's easy for you to talk. You're not in pain," he answered to my stunned disbelief. I promised to take him home that night, but before I could complete the arrangements he died.

Though there were always a few difficult patients, they were the exceptions. What was no exception was the patient brutalised by poverty, malnourished, depressed by unemployment, drained of self-respect, of privacy, of the basics of hygiene by overcrowding, and treated with contempt by the supposedly "caring" systems. That patient I knew. That patient was male, female, old, young and his tragic story involved nobody because it was just one tragedy out of tens of thousands. That's the way it is, ran the line. You have to accept things. There are some things you cannot change. Eventually, the rage stopped being vague and confused and solidified into determination inside me. It wasn't enough to be Dr. John, the local man who mopped up as best he could, mopped up the illnesses caused by deprivation. I was going to have to go back to the sources of those illnesses, and see what I could do to change them. Not singly or piecemeal. I had to change everything right now . . .

# Chapter 3

# A Foot in the Political Door

I have no orthodox set of beliefs, well thought out, interconnected. No dogma for all seasons. Instead I feel concern for particular cases, one of which is always obsessing me. I never choose an issue carefully for strategic reasons. There is always an initial gut-feeling, followed by action, and always total emotional involvement in the particular.

During my period as a general practitioner, the problems of unemployment, housing and poverty were constantly simmering in my mind and occasionally boiling over. The first time boiling point came, I wrote to the Archbishop. The second time, I wrote to a politician. At that stage, still completely ignorant as far as politics were concerned, I had no idea who was what in any of the parties. Nor, indeed, had I very much notion of the political philosophy of each party. I just knew that the Labour Party was supposed to care for working people, and so I sent off my letter.

> "The Leader" - (I didn't know his name)
> Labour Party,
> Dáil Eireann - (I didn't now the H.Q.)

Not long afterwards, a letter arrived from Brendan Corish, the leader at the time, suggesting that I should go along to a Labour Party Branch meeting in Eustace Street. Up to then, the nearest contact I had with the Labour Party was my ballot paper in the 1961 election. On that occasion, I had arrived to vote, only to find that there were Fianna Fáil canvassers, but none from the Labour Party. I went into the booth — no literature. Out again. Eventually, I found a leaflet on the floor, crisscrossed by the caterpillar tracks of dirty shoes, and on it, the name of the Labour candidate Frank Cluskey for whom I duly voted.

Now, I was taking one step nearer active involvement. I went to the meeting. There, I met Liam Hamilton, Proinsias Mac Aonghusa, Maire de Paor, broadcaster Jack Dowling and publisher Philip MacDermott, and listened, for the very first time, to the goings on at a political meeting, although perhaps "listened" is over-stating the case. I was up and down like a Jack-in-the-box, demanding to know what they were doing about one problem, what they proposed doing about another, and why they weren't making themselves felt about a third one. The people who were later to be my friends laughed at me in a bemused way.

"You're in too much of a hurry," they said. "You can't do things that way."

"But why," I asked, "why aren't you doing more about housing?"

"We're not doing it," someone said, "because we haven't got enough people like you — we can't do it all on our own."

It was the first of thousands of such meetings, and I fell on the new work with a positive hunger. Up to then, I had only attended medical meetings. Now, it was almost like being a student again — listening, reading, learning everything I could about reform of the economic situation, which in turn would make reform in the social sphere possible. For a considerable time, I became a passive listener, drinking it in, learning the political realities behind issues which I had known up to then only through personalities.

Eventually, Jack Dowling arranged that I should visit the Dáil to meet Michael Mullen, then Labour's only Dublin TD, and an official of the Irish Transport and General Workers' Union. Michael Mullen was a man about whom I had heard a great deal. I knew he had been born into a poor family and was largely self-educated and that he was an active trade unionist who had fought so hard for hotel workers. Up to his time, they had been working in appalling conditions. He organised them, fought for them, and by so doing, achieved a great name for himself. On meeting him, I thought he was a typical Dubliner. Short and squat. A concerned, serious face, slow to smile. I remember going to great trouble to make it clear to him that I came from a similar background, for fear that he might think I, being a doctor, had no place in the Labour Party. I felt honoured to be in his presence, especially since he was a TD, and faintly puzzled by the casual way he seemed to take being a parliamentarian. He talked of it as if it were of no consequence at all to him. It was obvious that his self-image was not tied up with being a member of the Dail.

Since that time, I have never had any cause to reconsider my high regard for Michael Mullen. He was a good friend to me, always ready to give advice when it was sought, sensible advice based on his long experience and intuition. Later on when attempts were made to have me expelled from the Labour Party, it was Michael Mullen who came to my rescue and scotched them. We had differences: he was a great Republican and had been imprisoned for his beliefs.

He did not go forward for re-election as a T.D. again because he felt he had a greater obligation to the trade union movement. He became General Secretary of the country's biggest union, the Irish Transport and General Workers Union. I think Michael Mullen left politics gladly, never having been enamoured of the Dáil, and believing that there was much more to be achieved within the trade union movement. I became his doctor, and later on, an honorary medical adviser to the Transport Union. In 1969, I applied to join the Union, and to my great pride, was accepted. I felt that to be a signal honour.

I worked with Michael Mullen on many issues. When the hunger strikers in Portlaoise were in a bad way, Mullen, myself, and that great humanitarian Senator Trevor West worked together on their behalf. Michael Mullen was a good man to work with, despite the fact that he never made an effort to be charming — he was blunt to the point of offending people, and even, at times, as Brendan Corish once commented, frankly cantankerous. But he was known as one of the few people in public life who was totally sincere, a real champion of the working classes, and a dedicated servant of his union.

A great deal of what I came to know about Michael Mullen was, of course, still to be discovered when I had that first meeting with him in the Dáil in November 1963 — a meeting made all the more exciting for me, a political novice, by the fact that the Turnover Tax Bill was being debated, and TDs were coming and going amid great noise and bustle. Nevertheless, he welcomed me warmly, and talked to me at length, finding out all about me and my reasons for becoming a member of the Party. Then he suggested I should be a candidate for the Labour Party in the next General Election. I was stunned, but, once I swallowed my surprise, excited and challenged by the idea. He introduced me to Brendan Corish in the Dáil.

"Dr. O'Connell is going to honour us by going forward in Dublin South-West, where he practises," Michael Mullen said.

"Sure we've too many candidates for Dublin South-West," Mr Corish said damply. I was enormously disappointed. I had expected the leader to be a tremendously warm and concerned man, and I felt he lacked the care for each individual member, which, to me, was the qualifying trait for a leader. If I were running a party, my major concern would be to make each member feel he belonged, feel he was important to the progress and development of the party.

However, Michael Mullen remained enthusiastic, telling me the facts of the constituency: that, for example, the highest Labour vote recorded there up to now was 743 votes. I decided that Mr Corish's indifference might be due to concern with the Turnover Tax bill which was creating a hectic atmosphere in the House, because of a rumour that two opposition deputies had been bought over by the Government. I thought I could recognise some of the faces, but relatively few.

Mullen told me to get in touch with a particular branch secretary in my area, which I duly did. We went to a pub and had a drink. We drank half our respective drinks before he spoke.

"You're a doctor?"

"Yes."

"Why would you want to join the Labour party?"

"I don't want to join. I'm already a member."

"Well, why would you want to come into this area?"

"Michael Mullen suggested it would be best as my medical practice is in this area."

Another long pause. We finished our drinks.

"Tell you what", he said, stuffing the ends of his scarf under his lapels, "Tell you what, we'll let you know."

Off he went, and that was the sum total of our contact. After a decent interval, I returned to Michael Mullen who gave me more names, but the result of my efforts was only slightly different. Eventually, I found a helpful and welcoming Branch Secretary in Myles O'Brien. My attempt to get into a branch where I might eventually be useful as a candidate had been an interesting exercise in "grassroots" politics, and had given me an understanding of how people can grow comfortable in failure. Some of the branch secretaries I met were happier to continue failing in election after election than to allow a new broom to get sweeping. I found out that they had held a meeting at which it was decided to keep me out, as an ambitious outsider.

Ambitious? New broom? Confessedly. Aggressively.

I went to work, attending branch meetings to organise the work of the branch, nagging, persuading, revitalising, and this time I was lucky; the people involved in the branch were happy to see something happening, cheered to be part of a bit of life and progress. I found that their methods were archaic, and wasteful of time, but within weeks, we had the whole thing streamlined. There was more discussion of policy, more running of fund-raising functions. I discovered that there was very little in the way of articulated Labour policy — just a tradition of championing the cause of the working man and the underprivileged. I found myself often in the situation of almost being afraid to ask for elucidation, for fear that somewhere all of the material I needed could be readily found, and that I was just too ignorant of the workings of the party to know where. Basically, what I found was that the party had a cap-and-muffler image, and that among its own devotees, the level of

60

understanding of what it was about and what it stood for was low indeed.

Then, in March 1965 the Taoiseach, Sean Lemass, dissolved the Dáil and called a General Election.

I still had connections with the first Labour branch whose meetings I had attended in Eustace Street and I went along to their selection conference, where Noel Browne was chosen as Labour candidate. To meet Noel Browne in person was itself a thrill. While I was still at school, I had heard my family talk of him, and he had assumed something of the proportions of a Saviour for me. We had been touched by TB and felt its consequences and here was a man who had done all any man could do to rid this country of TB. He was special to us but he also had the status of a historical figure in a way. The major controversies like the Mother and Child scheme had happened when I was quite young. I learned about them from others and from yellowing newspaper cuttings.

Getting to know Noel Browne as a man was a stimulating process. He is a man of much complexity, a complexity often denied by his friends and enemies. He has a tendency to polarise people, so that half those who know him see him as somewhere between the two. My own image of him is as Dorian Gray. Not that he has ever lived a life of debauchery — far from it —- but because he never seems to get any older, and he is always magnetic, utterly sincere, and a visionary. He is also a man of moods. One day he will meet you and charm you half out of your mind, the next he will cut you dead. In person, he is intense, very quietly spoken.

It has been said he cannot take disagreement, and that he will sever the relationships of years because of a disagreement. At Labour Party meetings, he would drive people crazy by speaking in this gentle voice of his, so low that he was virtually inaudible, and yet he's one of the most electrifying public speakers I have ever seen. And he operates an attraction (like gravity) on people who come within his orbit. This charismatic attraction also showed up most forcefully in his relationship with David Thornley, who first fell under the Browne spell in his teens and, was thereafter like a satellite — going far away

61

only to sweep back as close as ever.

It was Thornley who in 1973 proposed Noel Browne as a Trinity Senator, despite the fact that Thornley had spent months berating and criticising him. Noel Browne has always had that effect on people.

I can remember reading in the evening newspaper where a man and his wife and daughter of 16 years had been sentenced to six months imprisonment for breaking open the Poor Box in Francis Street church. Apparently, they had come down from Northern Ireland penniless, had sought help from the priests and had been refused. In desperation they broke open the Poor Box in the church and stole the contents — a mere 9/10d. The District Justice sentenced them, as I said, to six months imprisonment, while a younger daughter was sent to High Park Convent, Drumcondra. I thought the sentence was very harsh and I went down to the court with a view to getting them out on bail. I managed to see the District Justice in his chambers and made my request, telling him who I was. When he heard I was a Labour Party colleague of Noel Browne he was very sympathetic to my plea. It appears he was a victim of TB and Noel Browne was the great saviour. So Noel Browne unknowingly wielded influence everywhere, even in the Courts.

The interesting thing about Noel Browne is that although he is seen as a left-winger, the party that holds him in greatest esteem is probably Fianna Fáil, and I suspect that if he had stayed in Fianna Fáil, then he would have had a happier and more productive political career. Instead, he has spent many potentially productive years moving from party to party, in and out of the political wilderness. It is unfortunate. Here is a man of vast human concern, who has never had the chance to make that concern work in political terms over a long period of time, although even in the wilderness, he has a way of making other people work on his behalf, which means that his areas of concern never fade away.

During the earlier period when he was not in the Dáil and I was, he used to send me parliamentary questions to ask in the House. Our communication at that time was totally by means of letters, and so when we were both to speak at a meeting in Gaj's restaurant in Baggot Street, Dublin and arrived at the same time, he looked at me in a baffled way.

"Don't I know you from somewhere?" he asked. "Did we meet in some pub?"

Afterwards at the meeting, when he learned who I was, he was profuse in his apologies. Later, we worked together in great harmony in the Dáil and both of our names went on the very first Private Member's Bill on contraception, it having been agreed that this would not be a Labour Party motion, but that the two medical doctors in the Party should put their names to it.

I always tried to support him when Labour colleagues attacked him. There was an occasion when he made a speech in Waterford attacking the clergy in typical scathing Noel Browne fashion, and his speech gave great offence to a number of rural members of the Labour Party. The Parliamentary Party took exception to the speech. I defended him, pointing out that a great deal of what he had said was true. He was not at that meeting, but heard about it, and came to me later to murmur his thanks.

"They're savages, John," he said softly, "savages." He was referring of course, to some of his Labour colleagues.

What is so unusual about Noel Browne is not simply his capacity to make people adore him or hate him, but the fact that he can achieve both within a matter of minutes. The perfect example was the Labour Party Annual Conference of 1974 in Galway. He was at his best — and his worst. His speech was electrifying. He attacked the Coalition Government and the weakness of the Labour Ministers within it and was the great demagogue. He roused the audience to such a pitch of excitement that they would have marched for him then and there, to wherever he chose. But then he suddenly turned his attack on the Coalition into a vitriolic personal attack on Labour Party Leader, Brendan Corish. Within seconds, his words were drowned in a chorus of boos and he left the platform in defeat.

Noel Browne won the Labour Party nomination in the Artane constituency in 1977, but the Administrative Council of the Party refused to ratify his nomination and he was forced to fight the election as an Independent. He won convincingly, but once again, he was out in the political wilderness. After that election, I made a plea on radio that Noel and his colleagues be taken back into the party, that we needed the vitality of our own dissidents, and that, as Brendan Corish had once said, the Party should be an "orchestration of dissent." I failed. True, there was and is a widespread feeling that nobody can control Noel Browne. I believe that's nonsense. With a good leader, nobody is impossible to control.

At the Labour Party meeting in Eustace Street in March 1965 when Noel Browne was selected as the candidate in Dublin South East, I was introduced to him as a doctor, and I wished him luck. At the same meeting, it was decided that Proinsias Mac Aonghusa would run in County Louth, and half the branch announced their intention of going up there to support him. Someone asked me what I had planned. Nothing, I said. What could I have planned? Well hadn't my branch held a Selection Conference? No. Were they going to hold one? I didn't think so.

"Well go back up there fast and make them hold one."

Yessir. I returned to my branch and made noise.

We-ll, yes, they said. I suppose it wouldn't be a bad idea. Mmm. Yes. OK. Maybe.

"When?" This from me.

"Well, next week is St Patrick's Day, so we can't have a selection conference then. How about the week after?"

"The election is April the seventh!"

"Oh. Well?"

The imminence of the poll seemed to have no worries for them, but I pushed and hustled, and finally got them to hold their selection conference on Sunday afternoon. Each branch could send delegates, and it was a matter of finding a venue.

"God, yes," someone said, indecision melting them all over again like a heated jelly. "A venue. We didn't think of that."

"Listen," I said, "I've a house up there, and it has plenty of rooms we can use. There's your venue."

Once the last obstacle had been kicked out of the way, things began to get moving, notices were sent, and a crowd was expected.

Some of them would already have heard of me, since, on the advice of members, I had sent out a notice, letting people know that there would be local elections in June, and that I was interested in going forward for them as a candidate. Now, something like forty people gathered in my front room to make their decision, including one man who came in and began to bellow at me before the door had closed behind him.

Who the bloody hell was this John O'Connell, anyway, he wanted to know, and what was the meaning of this (waving it in the air) bloody letter, and how long had I been in the party, a wet weekend, and what was I but a bloody intruder and who did I think I was, God Almighty? I was staggered by the fury I had unwittingly aroused in this total stranger.

"I don't have to take this," I said to a friend who was pulling me out of the line of fire. "I'll tell them all to go to hell."

"Wait'll they select you, then tell them," my friend, Liam Reddy, who had a better sense of the theatre of the situation, advised. I waited. Three of us were selected.

"I'm sorry," I said, still mad as a wasp, "I'm not accepting the nomination. I don't want anything to do with this election."

One of the delegates cast a tired look at me.

"You have no say in the matter," he said, gathering up his papers briskly. "You've been selected, and that's all there is to it."

My hand was dragged from my side and shaken by the participants. My attacker left without a word. He had been most business-like about the whole thing, I thought. Breezed in, abused me, voted against me and then disappeared and never appeared in the election campaign. I soon wished that the rest of the Labour Party was as businesslike, if not quite so aggressive. At the first pre-election meeting, I had a chance to see the organisation in action, and the chance to do some calculations. What happened was that two canvassers went out, worked a little road I knew well, and reported back. Twenty houses done. All going well, Cheers, back pats. On the back of an envelope, I worked out the number done as against the number to do and the pace at which they were being done. The constituency could be properly covered, working at this pace-in fifteen months!

"Could I ask a question?" O'Connell, poised to throw a spanner in the works, "Did anyone know me in those houses?"

A glance between them.

"No, not as I remember, anyways."

I said nothing, but figured that something was going badly wrong, if an area thick with patients of mine didn't know me when canvassers went around. Or, more importantly, if, when those canvassers went around, my patients weren't ASKED if they knew me. Long thoughts. Quick decisions. I withdrew from that HQ and set up my own team of friends, family, and patients. The other candidate, seeing the efforts I was putting in, asked me why.

"Sure you won't get four hundred votes," he said.

"I'm in practice in this area," I responded. "And we've seven thousand patients between my partner and me. I can bank on three and a half thousand votes. I know my patients will vote for me."

"Oh, no, not at all," he said. "People just don't vote like that".

"I think they will."

Impasse.

The candidate, on second thoughts, decided to withdraw and was replaced by Dr John O'Donovan, Professor of Economics at UCD. Dr O'Donovan had a distinguished political career in Fine Gael, having been Parliamentary Secretary to a former Taoiseach, John A. Costello. However, due to some disagreement, he had quit Fine Gael and joined Labour.

He preferred to operate in that part of Dublin South West Constituency in which he was well known from previous elections — Ranelagh, Rathmines and adjoining areas — and was able to muster a massive team of university students for his campaign.

My team operated in the dense housing districts of Kimmage, Crumlin and Drimnagh. I knew that I was up against tough opposition which included Fine Gael's Richie Ryan and Fianna Fáil's Noel Lemass, in an area which had, up to then,

66

never had a Labour seat. I worked hard, too, although I found the face to face canvassing for support intensely uncomfortable. I would often find myself finishing a chat with a patient or a friend on the street, and realise as I walked away that I had not asked for his or her support, nor even told them I was going forward as a candidate. But I pushed myself and did it and found it easier in reality than in theory. People were kind to me, and warm. By election day, we were all exhausted but guardedly hopeful, although we knew that a victory for Labour would startle most of the politicians and pundits.

The Labour Party final rally was at the G.P.O. and I was on the platform behind Brendan Corish, who orated at length about the Labour Party and its various candidates. When he came to Dublin South West, he said;

".. and in Dublin South West, we have a great person in Dr John ....O'Donovan."

I was greatly disheartened by the fact that the Party Leader was evidently unaware of my candidature and my confidence was badly shaken on the very eve of the poll.

Election day was April seventh, and on that day, when I went to vote, I knew I'd made it. Something I have always been able to gauge, is the depth of feeling in a crowd, especially a crowd on election day. The signs are unmistakable — the thumbs up, the nods, the winks, the quick squeeze of your elbow leaves you in no doubt. But in this, my first election, how could I be sure? The following day, I had my initial experience of seeing at first hand the counting of the votes. I was also to meet for the first time Noel Lemass, son of the then Taoiseach and Fianna Fáil's front runner in the constituency. It was early in the count.

"How is it going?" I asked him.

"Oh, our figures show that Labour has won a seat," he said, rather surprised, "and it looks like this fellow O'Connell will get it."

Little did he know at that moment that I was "this fellow O'Connell."

The returning officer was just chalking up the result of the first count:

Noel Lemass        7596

67

| | |
|---|---|
| Richie Ryan | 5484 |
| Joe Dowling | 4607 |
| Ben Briscoe | 4416 |
| Jim O'Keeffe | 4352 |
| John O'Connell | 4299 |

Noel Lemass romped home on the first count while I had to wait a nerve-racking thirteen hours to hear that Noel's prediction proved true: I won the second seat in this five-seat constituency with a final vote of 8500. The remaining three seats were won by Richie Ryan, Ben Briscoe and Joe Dowling.

Noel Lemass was a politician without guile whose greatest handicap in public life was the fact that he was the son of such a national figure as Sean Lemass. Also, Noel was never one to engage in the sort of petty one-upmanship which can too often be the curse of constituency politics. His untimely death in 1976 came as a blow to his political friends and foes alike.

I was a TD before they ever counted the votes and announced that I had come in second in a five seat constituency. Oddly enough, my election was not the thrill I expected — nothing like the excitement and pride involved in becoming a doctor. Then, the first day you were addressed as "Doctor," you felt ten feet tall, you had status. Being a TD was rewarding and a relief after the hard work, and that was it. I promptly sent around a letter to all those who had helped me, saying thanks, and telling them that I would shortly set up a series of advice centres. If I expected a welcome, what I met with was ferocious hostility. I was arraigned before the Labour Party Constituency Council and asked to explain my letter, and it was stated that if such advice centres were to be set up, it would be by the Council itself. I tried, as patiently as I could, to explain that this was one of the services for the provision of which I had been elected — something they mightn't be aware of as they hadn't had a TD before.

The hostility simmered, heated from below by the still existing resentment at this "outsider" who had been elected against all the odds. It bothered me. Any kind of criticism bothers me. I have never been able to understand those politicians who get a buzz out of being attacked, who laugh and say, "Ah, sure any publicity is good publicity." If something bad is written in the paper about me, I worry about it. If something bad is written which is also inaccurate, I boil and seethe. In one sense, this is a disadvantage. A hard neck and a deaf ear make for solid nights of restful sleep. In another sense, it is an advantage. I never take anything for granted, never blunder along offending people without thinking, or because I feel above criticism. I simply listen and react to everything I hear.

The great cushion against the hostility of this early stage, however, was the fact that there I was at the gates of Dáil Eireann, buoyed up by a sense of mission, convinced that I was going to change, if not the world, then certainly a spoonful of it called Ireland. For one thing, I was going to change the dispensary system, that mincing machine grinding the dignity, the self respect and the natural health out of people. I wanted people to have a choice of doctor, instead of the routine which saw them crowded into cold, damp, old, depressing dispensaries, huddled on benches, waiting for the inattention of some overworked part-time doctor who couldn't cope, and as a result, constantly vented his frustration on the patients by his contemptuous manner and in snappy little outbursts. I had hopes on this issue, since in the early days of that Dáil, Donough O'Malley, the Minister for Health, accosted me and told me he planned to be a truly reforming minister.

"You slag me about anything you want done," he said, with what I thought was amazing openness. "You slag me and I'll do it."

Admittedly, that was one of the few positive notes in the early days of my apprenticeship to the Dáil. The main problem was that nobody thought of the Dáil as something you needed to be taught about, and so we newcomers arrived without the smallest clue as to how this impressive machine worked. The ignorance manifested itself in awkward little mistakes. I was last to sign in on my first day, although I'd been among the first to arrive, because I didn't know that you had to sign in, let alone where. I also committed the error of sitting on the Fianna Fáil side in the Dáil restaurant, something which is generally not done as there is an unwritten rule that members of different parties generally sit in separate areas. Why this should be so, I have never been able to ascertain. Generally, I spent the first few months in the Dáil groping — groping through the administrative, social and emotional entanglements it presented. During that time, my life-savers were the ushers — particularly Peadar Lawless — unfailingly kind and helpful, and all-knowing about the workings of that complex institution.

One month to the day after I entered the Dáil a major bus strike began. The issues, at this distance, have faded from my mind, but what I do remember is that the strike dragged on and on and nobody seemed to be doing anything about it. People were walking and complaining, but the strike dragged on despite the inconvenience it was causing. When I was outside the Dáil, I had written to a politician to get action on some issue. It seemed to me that the logical extension of that was to do something myself now that I was a TD. Because the prime movers in the dispute were from a breakaway union, the Labour Party did not want to get caught in the pincers of breakaway versus regular union. I knew practically nothing about unions, and sailed into the dispute on a wave of optimistic ignorance. When the leaders of the breakaway union visited the Dáil they were ignored by the Labour Party. I was the only one who was accessible and so they talked to me, explaining that they were eager to go back to work, but could get no body to listen to them. I took them into the public gallery while the bus strike was under discussion at Question Time, and they stolidly listened as a Minister replied to one query with a "Let's all ignore this and perhaps it will go away" sort of answer.

I then phoned the Chairman of CIE. He was out playing golf, I was told. I rang the Labour Court, talked to Dermot McDermott, the Conciliation Officer, and told him that these people were eager to get the thing sorted out, and when could he see them? I offered my house as a possible venue, and that night, the leaders of the breakaway union and Dermot McDermott met in the house, talked until four a.m., and at the end of it, a statement was issued, the men went back to work, and Dublin was able to get about that morning by bus.

When I went into the Labour party rooms in the Dáil that day, there was a standing ovation for me. I couldn't believe it, any more than I could believe the encomiastic editorial in the "Irish Times", and the fact that John Healy devoted much of his Backbencher column to the work of this "young deputy from Dublin South-West."

Talk about being drunk with power! I thought there was nothing I could not do. I put down questions by the thousand in the Dáil. As a new broom, I was in danger of wearing myself down to the bristles, and everybody else along with me. Now, looking back, I wish I could do it again, or perhaps find someone as enthusiastic and hard-working as I was and channel their energies, train them, help them to focus on the things that matter, instead of the million and one things that distract you from that vital point. The point is that a hard-working and concerned opposition Deputy can make sure we have a good government, by keeping the Ministers on their toes, using adjournment debates to the full, putting down the right kind of questions at the right time, understanding and using the Committee system. I realised the importance of this too late, and was often astonished to realise how poor the opposition tended to be on strategy.

Time and again I would be told — "Go in there and say something on 'X'". And I would know practically nothing about X, but it was regarded as important to keep the flag flying, to be seen as saying something and to be part of the wheels going round. I remember asking at some stage what research facilities we had as a party, and getting blank looks, because it was simply not seen as important that you should, if you spoke, have thoughtful and properly researched things to say.

All of which sounds as if I were becoming disillusioned, which at this time was not the case. I was in the grip of a missionary zeal, and the odd poke here or there was not going to push me off the path. I would almost literally have laid down my life for the Labour Party. I was determined that we take over the reins of government, and had supporters calling every night to work out how and when and what we should be doing. In this I was extremely lucky. My supporters were not just used for the election. They were part of my continuing work and thought. All the time, the twin concerns in my mind were health and housing, housing and health, the two sores I encountered daily in my work as a doctor.

Not long after the bus strike had been solved, various TDs were asked to go down to Griffith Barracks, where homeless women and their children were being housed. At the time, married couples in furnished flats had no security of tenure. Once the baby arrived, they could be, and were, dumped without hope of finding somewhere else and so they became homeless. Instant stigma accompanied that label of homelessness.

The wives and children were taken into Griffith Barracks, the husbands were expected to stay in city lodging houses. Grimmer places than the barracks would have been hard to create for women and children. They lived in big dormitories, locked in by great gates that clanked, and which were topped by barbed wire. It looked like a mini-Belsen by the Canal at Harold's Cross Bridge. Bad enough as the separation of husband and wife was, it was made immeasurably worse by the implementation of rules, such as the one which ensured that if a man missed his bus from work in the evening, and arrived late, the gates were kept locked and communication with his wife was permitted only through the wire. The couple had to stand to talk over the doings of their day in the rain, poking fingers through the wire. Eventually, the men baulked, and said they weren't going anywhere, that they were locking themselves in the Barracks and staying put.

This was when they asked the TDs to come and meet them. The TDs listened to them and went home. I came, listened, and stayed, arriving every day to help fight what I felt was an appalling injustice. I cared deeply, and I went about showing it in what I now realise were totally wrong ways.

I first of all cobbled everybody I knew in the Dáil for help, ploughing into political friends and foes alike with the subtle grace of a driverless bulldozer.

"But you know what kind of people the Griffith Barracks people ARE," one TD said to me, his face warped with distaste.

"It doesn't matter if they were every last one of them murderers," I stormed. "It's their basic human rights as people we're talking about, not their suitability as dinner guests or whatever you're thinking about. They're people. They have rights. And they're being treated like animals."

I issued statements attacking the Minister for Health, Donough O'Malley, whose responsibility it was. I tried to get a housing aid committee off the ground — vainly, as it turned out. The Labour Party watched my antics with silent distaste, which at the time disappointed me bitterly.

Here was a burning issue, housing, which was at the root of almost all of Dublin's social problems. Here was a situation which pointed up that issue in a particularly human and painful way. Here was an opportunity, I thought, to show what we were about, to act on our principles. As it was, I was virtually on my own, buzzing like a bee in a jam-jar, trying to find a way out. And, like the bee, I stung everybody who came near me.

Because of my role in solving the bus strike, the board of directors of Arthur Guinness Son & Company (Dublin) Ltd., arranged a lunch in my honour and I used the occasion to ask them to support my idea of a housing aid society, telling them breezily that I'd forego the lunch if they'd do so. I was not a wild success. Friends pointed out that at meetings in support of the Griffith Barracks people, attended by me, there were known communists, and suggested that the homeless people were being exploited by others for varying reasons. Possibly true, I said, but I recalled Churchill's remark when Hitler invaded Russia and Churchill had to say supportive things about Stalin. He said then that if Hitler invaded hell, he would find it in himself to say something good about the Devil. In the same way, I was for anybody who was for these unfortunate people.

In discussions with Proinsias Mac Aonghusa, then Vice-Chairman of the Labour Party and the only major Labour figure to come to my aid, the notion of sending a telegram to the Pope surfaced, God alone knows from where. The theory behind it was that the Pope was visiting the United Nations and so was the Taoiseach Sean Lemass, and if we sent a telegram to the Pope, it would severely embarrass the Government and action might be taken on the problem. We drafted the telegram and worked out the list of people and newspapers who were due to receive copies. Then we parted, and I set off home, where I was a victim of cold feet. At ten thirty that night, overwhelmed by a gut feeling that this would be a massive mistake, I phoned Proinsias.

"Hey, listen Proinsias," I said. "I'm having second thoughts about the telegram thing."

"Why?"

"It just feels wrong to me. I really don't know why. But I really would prefer if you didn't send it."

"Oh."

"You won't, will you?"

"Not if you don't want me to."

End of conversation. I woke on Saturday morning, and phoned Proinsias.

"I'm really relieved we didn't go ahead with the telegram business," I said. "I'm more convinced than ever that it would have been a mistake."

"What do you mean, didn't go ahead with it? I sent it as we arranged."

"Oh, God, no! But I phoned you last night and asked you not to."

"I don't remember talking to you last night. I must have answered in my sleep."

A sinking feeling began inside me, portent of what was to come. And what was to come was one of the most embarrassing periods of my political life. The Sunday papers were a nightmare in black type. I got them on that Saturday night, fresh off the press, leaving black smears on my fingers and black marks on my soul. "DUBLINER'S APPEAL TO THE POPE" said the *Sunday Independent*. What everybody else said I would prefer to forget, if only I could. My skin still crawls at the memory of it. I felt it looked cheap, opportunistic, naive and vulgar. Which was nothing to what some people, like those in Dublin Corporation, felt it looked like. The Corporation met in emergency session specifically to condemn me. My one consolation was that the Dáil was not in session, and I hoped that by the time it re-assembled, some of the heat would have died down.

In fact, I was not to be so lucky. Donough O'Malley summoned me to the Custom House to meet him, and bullied me unmercifully in front of his aides and two stenographers, who occasionally, as the diatribe spewed over their bowed heads, cast me small quiet glances of sympathy. O'Malley was a big, handsome, imposing man, and I felt literally sickened with dismay when he pounded on his desk and asked how dare I do what I had done. Then he dismissed the stenographers and the aides, and closed the door behind them.

"John," he said with a grin, "That was just for their benefit. OK?"

And I took it. Retrospectively, I was furious with myself, but I was a political pygmy, and knew no better. Some years later when another Minister for Health, Erskine Childers summoned me into his presence to clip my wings over another campaign I was waging, things were very different, and the hand pounding the table was mine, but that's another story.

The whole Griffith Barracks episode began to take on the quality of a nightmare. Each way I turned to try to pull myself and the others out of it, I simply got in deeper. The thing began to develop a surreal undertow. They were going to blow up Nelson's Pillar. Or rather, they were going to drill it to pieces with the drills you use to dig up roads. They had the drills and the extension power leads. *That* would show them, they confided in my ear, showing me printed leaflets they planned to scatter from the top of the Pillar in which they said that I had done my best, but nobody was listening, and they had decided that the only way to solve their problem was by taking action themselves. Drilling Nelson. I thought about it. They meant it. There was some unfortunate man guarding the gate at the bottom of the Pillar, whose job presumably entailed repelling boarders. If he did his job, they would, in their frustration, half kill him. Or worse, whole kill him. That I couldn't countenance; I phoned Dublin Castle, and told the activists I was ringing Dublin Castle, and the plan fell through.

Next on the agenda was an occupation of the grounds of the Archbishop's Palace. I vetoed it. Now that was a great mistake. The best thing they could have done was to occupy the Archbishop's grounds, had I but the wit to see it at the time. He would have had to ask them in, and the publicity wouldn't have done him any harm, and action would have resulted. In the end some personal friends and I organised finance to purchase caravans and we finally got the homeless families to a site. One of the biggest contributors to our fund was Fianna Fáil TD, P. J. Lenihan, father of Minister Brian Lenihan, who took a most couragous stand in support of these homeless people at the very time that I was in conflict with his government. It was, however, an unsatisfactory end for the Griffith Barracks homeless and for me and for the housing problem, and I was stupified by anger and frustration. I was also beginning to realise that good intentions and a vigorous attack don't always solve everything. I wouldn't say that the experience turned me into a subtle politician. It just changed me from being an elephant in a china shop to being a bull in a china shop.

Nor did the controversy die down as quickly as I had hoped. A year or more later, when O'Malley was now Minister for Education, there was a major debate in the Dáil on the place of the Church in Education. Things had reached an extremely contentious point, when O'Malley cut through the cross talk and, fixing me with a wicked eye, said, "A Cheann Comhairle, I propose that we send a telegram to the Pope." There was uproar in the Dáil, and I sat there burning and hoping that a natural disaster would sweep me out of it. Paddy Lindsay, then a Fine Gael TD, came to my aid and defused the situation a little.

"The Minister may look like Bob Hope," he muttered, just loud enough to be heard, "but there's no reason for him to act like him."

Fortunately, I was kept so busy with my medical work and my constituency work that I had little time to brood over the early Dáil mistakes. My patients needed me, and my constituents needed me, and the fact that I had embarrassed myself by making a couple of tactical errors was, to them, neither here nor there. During my first years in the Dáil, I was also building up my political "clinic," and coming to terms with the personal conflict caused by my medical work. The first was one of the aspects of my political work I have always found most rewarding, and at the same time, most frustrating. Most rewarding, because sometimes you can help people, and you help them in a face to face way which is very satisfactory.

Take the case of one man who had lived with his parents, on and off, and when his father died, received an order to quit the house. He came to me, to see what I could do, and I went into Dublin Corporation and had the rules read to me. No hope, said the person reading the rules. The man had to have lived in the house continuously for the past four years ... No Go, I admitted. But then came a second part of the ruling, and he fitted that. The man stayed in his house. Satisfaction all round.

In many cases, however, it was dissatisfaction all round. Dissatisfaction when I would have to tell a couple that no matter what hopeful noises had been made at them, and no matter how they had lulled themselves into thinking that their points would ensure them a house, they had no real chance at all. I have always felt it my duty to tell people the truth in these situations, and not just to give them soft soap. What's the point? Knowing the truth can be a deeply depressing experience, true. The eyes acknowledge it and the face softens into despair. But at least when you have kicked the pointless hope out from under people, with any sort of luck, you can put a bit of fight into them, and can then help them to find some solution to their individual portion of our appalling housing problem, or to find some loophole which will ameliorate their situation temporarily.

If there was a graph of my medical practice and my political "clinic", the lines over the first months in the Dáil would climb up like the side of the Sugarloaf mountain. As a GP who was also a TD, I faced a problem of conscience. The Labour party, as one of the major planks in its policy, held that there was an urgent necessity for a free medical service. I fully supported that policy.

How then could I happily proceed with a medical practice in which I took money from people? Not on. I could not rub those two incompatibles together and hope they would get smoother with time. So I stopped charging patients. The problem was that then my practice simply split its sides. I often had the impression that patients were coming from Belfast and Wexford to my clinic, and I often worked from two in the afternoon until ten at night without so much as a break for a cup of tea. It was obvious that this could not go on, and so I gave up general practice. With regret. But I had a feeling that, while in general practice I could give personal, immediate help to people with problems, as a politician I could perhaps solve some of the problems which were at the root of my patients' difficulties.

One of the reasons for this conviction was the fact that increasingly, I found that what I was doing was social medicine — offering tranquillisers to people suicidally depressed because of their real problems with overcrowding, or lack of money, or dearth of work — and I knew that I would end up despising myself if I didn't stop. It was like offering aspirins to the victims of an earthquake. I was going to have to see what I could do about the earthquake.

# Chapter 4

# Thalidomide: The Damaged Children

The Thalidomide story had begun in 1958, long before I became a TD. It was the wonder drug. Available without prescription, it was so harmless, so safe. No need for doctors to oversee who was taking it. Sure you couldn't do yourself any more damage than if you were swallowing Smarties. The perfect tranquilliser for the uptight. The perfect hypnotic for the sleepless. Virtually impossible to overdose with it. Safe for mothers and babies. I hated it from the word go.

When the company's rep called on me to recommend this new panacea, I was hostile.

"It's a hypnotic, right."

"Yes, and it's also . . ."

"If it's a hypnotic, it should be on prescription."

Long pause. Then a small, assured smile.

"Well, Dr O'Connell, we don't really care whether or not you prescribe it, we can't supply enough of it to fill the demand."

The wonder drug. Still a wonder drug here when the reports of ghastly distorted little bodies began to filter through from other countries. Distaval, a terrible drug, was causing these things. So sad. Aren't we lucky we have this marvellous thing called Softenon.

Except that the two were *one and the same drug* — Thalidomide, under different names but with equally destructive effects. The destructive effects were unequalled in any pharmaceutical disaster up to that time — or indeed by anything since. Babies died. The ones who survived had limbs missing. No arms. Just fingers growing out of their shoulders. No legs. Some had no ears. A few doctors in different countries began to combine the incidents into a ghastly pattern.

Thalidomide was fingered as being responsible. Up to that point, it had been a disaster. Now, it was a disaster compounded in this country by criminal negligence on the part of the manufacturers who merely required that doctors in Ireland be sent a circular in January 1962 stating that the drug had been withdrawn. They did not scour the pharmacies and shops for remaining stocks — just circularised doctors. Three years later, I was able to buy Thalidomide over the counter of a chemist's shop in this country, without the use of a prescription. *Three years after* the alarming cases in Britain. *Three years after* the reports of disastrous deformities.

It was criminal negligence, too, on the part of our Department of Health who failed to take any measures to have the drug withdrawn, or alert people to the dangers of leftover supplies in their homes. In Ireland some of the evidence suggested that a few of the victims might have been born perfect had the alarm been raised in time.

I became aware and in 1971 I inevitably became involved. I took on the cases of the Irish Thalidomide children and set up the Association for Justice for them using my office as headquarters. I visited Jack Ashley, the British M.P. who had done so much to make the British aware of the damage the drug had done. At home, we carried out our own campaign. At the beginning we concentrated on investigating the issue and encouraging those who were victims of the drug. We reached people who had coped, baffled, with this apparent act of God, never connecting it with the wonder drug Thalidomide taken in pregnancy. We found a mother with a deaf and deformed child — a classic Thalidomide victim — in the School for the Deaf on the Navan Road. She never knew anything about the drug and would have struggled all her life to support the unfortunate child without help or compensation.

I became emotionally involved and furious at the lack of care being given to these children and their parents, and made a great deal of noise about it, which resulted in January 1972 in a summons to the office of the Minister for Health. I, remembering another summons from a predecessor, Donough O'Malley and the humiliation of it, prepared like a CIA man going to stay in Moscow. With two secretaries, one on either side of me, I went to meet Minister Erskine Childers. He refused to allow them in. Fury gave me courage and I ploughed into his office and banged on the desk. It was not good enough, the way this big German company, Chemie Grunenthal, was being let get away with  ruining the lives of so many Irish people, and he, as Minister for Health, was going to have to accept responsibilities and do something about it. Right now, he was going to have to start to right the great wrong.

"Minister, I think you should go to Germany to see these Chemie Grunenthal people on behalf of the Irish victims."

He was cold.

"I won't Deputy".

"Well, if you won't, then I will".

Within a week I was off to Germany. I had never been near Germany before, and for all I remember of it as a place, I might as well never have been there that time, either. The German Government paid for my trip — partly, I believe, as a PR gesture — and I was given an itinerary, which would have absorbed my time in being whisked around and gazing at shiny new clinics for this and that. I tore it up. If there was one fact-finding mission which required me, more than any other, to be free of the buffering and cotton wool of other people's press-agentry, this was it. I pursued instead Franz Wirtz the head of Chemie Grunenthal, manufacturers of the Thalidomide drug, getting him on the phone at his home in the middle of the night.

No, no, he said sleepily, no point in our meeting, it was nothing to do with him. All out of his hands.

The words had a smooth glibness from over-use.

"I will meet you," I said, rawly determined, "if I have to stand outside the gates of your factory or your castle for the next month."

He eventually agreed to see me, giving me such rapid-fire instructions that I was sure he hoped I would take a wrong road and end up in Lapland. We were to meet at Stolberg, a little town on the Belgian/German frontier, two hundred miles away. A fast German Government car took me there, and we met at a little restaurant. Very civilised. Very persuasive. Both he and his legal adviser Herr Wartenslieben spoke perfect English. If I would just call off my campaign, all would be well.

He showed me documents, which reinforced my belief that our Department of Health had been more sinning than sinned against, and, realising its criminal negligence, had done a cover-up job. I made sure that Franz Wirtz and his legal adviser, Herr Wartensliebe knew that John O'Connell was:

a) A doctor who fully understood the ins and outs of the case.
b) A politician with sufficient independence to fight this thing through, regardless of Government support at home, or lack of it.
c) Not to be bought.

C) was important as the Thalidomide case is a sad record of the corruptibility of campaigners, bought off by the vast money machines of the pharmaceutical industry.

Before I left Germany, a meeting of the Thalidomide Foundation (set up by the German Government to disburse the compensation monies to the victims) was held, with John O'Connell knocking politely for admittance as arranged. A heavy came to the door. "I am sorry. No one here speaks English." I looked past him and saw in the shadows the legal adviser Herr Wartenslieben whom I had spoken to the day before.

"That man speaks perfect English," I said, pushing by him, trailed by Ray Doyle and Seamus Counihan of Independent Newspapers and John Kelly of the *Sunday Press*. I was determined to ask the relevant, impertinent questions that needed to be asked. The chairman, a silver-haired authoritarian in his seventies, went puce with fury.

"How dare you come over from Ireland to ask such things?" he bellowed. "You will not be permitted . . ."

"I didn't know the Gestapo still operated here." I was hitting below the belt. But it worked. He suddenly became cooperative.

I talked of how shabbily they had treated the Irish Thalidomide cases, indicated new moves to meet their indifference, and was sickened to realise they knew so much. They had spies in all of the Thalidomide campaign camps.

On January 12 1973, I left Germany knowing and understanding much, but uneasy because of the number of eminent people who had apparently become corrupted and were living indirectly off the fight for crippled youngsters. Uneasy, too, because of the incredible extent of the cover-up. Faked clinical trials were submitted to a reputable American medical journal that later realised the truth. I was determined to go back again. But at home, there was much to do. For one thing, we needed to identify the children who were genuinely maimed by the Thalidomide drug, and separate them from unfortunates damaged by some other agent.

But within two days of my return a General Election was called by the Taoiseach, Jack Lynch. I had already arranged for two German Thalidomide experts — Professors Lenz and Marquandt — to examine the Irish children suspected of being victims of the drug, and they arrived on polling day, February 28. Professors Lenz and Marquandt set up a day's tests at the Children's Hospital, Crumlin. We needed to show the German Government that their law setting up the Thalidomide Foundation, which was passed apparently in the smug belief that Ireland would kow-tow to it, did not bind us or limit our demand for compensation in any way.

This German law had, I found, been passed without a cheep from the Irish Government. It committed children of different nationalities including the Irish to a miserable settlement and deprived them of their rights to sue the company. At this time, the Department of Health seemed to rely on weakly obstinate inaction, acquiescence and silence. For example, they had a study done on Softenon, the Irish brand of Thalidomide, but wouldn't release what it said. The Department absorbed information and did nothing with it. When I asked, for example, why nothing had been done about the German law disenfranchising Irish victim children, I was told that the Irish

83

Embassy in Bonn had been made aware of the content of the German Act. Full stop. Information absorbed, no action.

For the parents trying to cope, it was ghastly. There was no medical service designed to help them. Many of them suffered financial hardship trying to get artificial limbs fitted. The emotional trauma was massive.

I asked the Labour Party for permission to put down a motion on the Dáil Order Paper calling on the Minister for Health to compensate the Thalidomide children. I was told by the Labour Party hierarchy that I would be given permission provided that I agreed to place Brendan Corish's name over mine on the motion. I said I didn't care whose name was on it provided it got under way. It took its place on the Dáil Order Paper and in the interim, the General Election took place. Within three weeks Brendan Corish became Minister for Health and he found himself in a position to honour the commitment we had sought in the motion.

Honour it he did. He awarded to each of the thirty-three victims a lump sum equivalent to four times that granted by the German Government, and he supplemented the German Government's monthly allowance to these children by an equivalent amount. This meant that a child totally maimed and incapacitated could receive as much as £16,000 by way of lump sum with an additional monthly allowance for life of £75. Arguably the most gross aspect of the case was the bizarre points system the German company put in place to cope with compensation claims and limit them so as not to erode their profits. If a child had thighs cut short by over half on one side, that child got 10 points. Complete blindness earned 60 points, as did an inoperable heart condition. Ten points went for an ear missing or a cleft palate; 100 points qualified a child for 25,000DM, the equivalent of £3,980.

The directors of the parent company should have gone to jail, but they dragged out the action and brought in battalions of highly paid lawyers to find loopholes in every relevant law.

One interesting aspect of the Thalidomide saga was the stance taken by the Irish media from the time the scandal became public. Perhaps most puzzling was the stance taken by the *Irish Times* as evident from an article, "Babies Without Limbs", by their medical correspondent Dr Alfred Byrne on July 14, 1962.

This is it:

> Behind the *Irish Times* recent disclosure that a pharmaceutical preparation named Softenon,which is one name for the drug Thalidomide had been withdrawn from sale last December because of possible harmful side-effects lies one of the most significant and moving medical stories of our time. I had thought to tell it in the final page of typescript meant for an article entitled "Avoidable Misconceptions" which was published here on January 15th but it was decided editorially to delete that particular page — a decision which I respect — because its contents were then considered too alarming to make public. For that reason, Thalidomide was deliberately not named in a piece which appeared in May on "Testing New Drugs."
>
> THE FACTS
> Now, however, the essentials of the Thalidomide story are common property. Apart from what appeared in the newspaper, those of our readers who see the British press will be aware that it has printed numerous news reports, features and accounts of "campaigns" relating to what has happened over the drug in several countries, including our own. The question was this week raised as an issue of national importance in both Houses of Parliament. So I feel that far from doing any harm, publication of certain of the facts at this stage may even do some good.

In 1971, when the compensation awards for the British victims gave new impetus to the Irish campaign, it was Ray Doyle of the *Evening Herald* who pursued every avenue of approach on behalf of the Irish Thalidomide children, and it was to him, perhaps, that most credit was due for the success of the campaign.

What success there was, was limited and tainted. I met one of the German doctors, Dr Schriber, who had campaigned on behalf of the children there. He told me that when he reached agreement with the drug company to compensate the children they had a dinner that night celebrating it. He was with the directors of the drug company at the dinner and the waiter came over and told him he was wanted on the phone. When he went over, he found the phone call actually was not for him — it was for a director of the drug company. But before he could make it clear to the caller that he had the wrong man, the caller — a German Government Minister, asked "Did you get the doctor to sign the agreement document?" The bottom line, as far as the doctor was concerned, was that Government and big business had been working together in the effort to minimise the compensation paid to the most grossly damaged children.

We learned from the Thalidomide disaster. We learned never to prescribe drugs for women in pregnancy if a prescription could be avoided, if a problem could be coped with by any other means. We learned that caution in authorising drugs (as is often criticised in the US approach) can save lives and misery. We learned that the most damaged children can grow into resourceful self-reliant adults with an undamaged capacity for love and for trust.

But the lesson was dealt out with corruption and cruelty.

**The Election Count — Dublin South-West Constituency,
8 April 1965**

*Left to right* - Noel Lemass, Ben Briscoe, Dr. John O'Connell,
Joe Dowling. Seated is a count official.

Dr John O'Connell with Senator Ted Kennedy at the U. S.
Senate Sub-Committee hearings on Northern Ireland, 1972

Dr John O'Connell with Harold Wilson,
14 March 1972

**At the Fianna Fail Árd-Fheis, 1985,**
*Left to right* - Rory O'Hanlon, Dr John O'Connell, Brendan Daly

**Dr John O'Connell in Ceann Comhairle Robes, 1982**
*Photo courtesy of "Aspect" Magazine*

**With the Fianna Fáil leader, Charles Haughey, 1985**

# Chapter 5

# A Coalition of Personalities

At first they were names, these Labour Party colleagues. Names with soft focus faces attached to them. They gradually came into sharper focus and I developed reactions to them.

The leader in '65 was Brendan Corish, who I think would have had a much happier life if he had been a backbencher, and had spent most of his time in Wexford walking his dog and talking to his friends. His election as leader, and continuing hold on the office, were the triumph of popularity over suitability. He was, and is, a very kind, sensitive man of occasional warmth. I remember being told that he had become so friendly with his driver while a Minister in the Coalition Government of the Fifties, that he afterwards always stayed with him when in Dublin. It would not be untypical of him. I remember asking him once what it was like for him being Minister for Social Welfare during the disastrous coalition of 1954-57.

"John I used to lie awake at night, worrying about the unemployed," he said.

"Brendan," I retorted, unable to resist. "Brendan, the difference between you and me is that I would sleep at night — and I'd do something about them during the daytime."

Comments like that never seemed to reach or change him, although he could be hurt quite easily on occasion, and was shy and suspicious, especially of newspaper people. I felt he always wanted to keep them at bay.

I think he was unhappy from the moment he became leader,

and would have been happier if he could have resigned, as he so often threatened to do. But each time, he was prevailed on by members of the Party's hierarchy and this constant threat- and-persuasion crisis was very unsettling in its effect on the Party.

I was sorry for him, recognising the fact that he was a man who had been pushed into a role in which he was unhappy, not just in internal Party matters but even in external relations.

The sad paradox was that although Brendan Corish was in many ways unhappy with the Party leadership, in other ways he enjoyed it. And, particularly during his two spells as a Coalition Minister, he relished having civil servants about him. A year after the second Coalition was defeated, he told me that he had difficulty remembering that Mr Haughey now held his government job.

"Whenever I hear on the radio 'the Minister for Health,' I turn and cock my ear," he smiled.

Back in opposition after the Coalition Government of 1973 to 1977 he would sit on the Dáil benches and point out particular civil service advisers with Haughey, and tell me how he knew one or had this one or that one work for him. Once he even asked Haughey if he might talk with his advisers — just for old time's sake.

Of course, in 1965, I had no old times to think about. Not only was I new and unknown, I was apparently not very individual, either; on one of my first days in the Dáil the then Fianna Fáil leader, Sean Lemass, mistook me for Frank Cluskey who was the new Labour TD in Lemass's constituency, put his arm around me and drew me with him into the voting lobby. This was so unexpected a mistake that I was struck dumb, and went lamblike to vote for something about which I hadn't a clue, and to which my party was probably opposed.

Frank Cluskey impressed me from the first time I met him as a man whose political smarts were unique. He manoeuvred individuals and blocks of individuals in a choreography that never became apparent until after the event and that merited fascinated applause unless (as happened to me a couple of times) you happened to be scrunched in the process.

I cannot believe that Frank Cluskey ever had a naive

moment, whereas at times I believe I suffer from chronic ingrown political naivete. Quite early on in my days in the Dáil, for instance, I discovered that my plans for solving the housing problem would be very much at odds with Trade Unions: they would not want to see a massive housing plan because, although it would mean massive employment in the short term, in the longer term, it would put their members out of work for perhaps a decade. I didn't realise that; I thought we could just solve the housing problem. If there was coverage of the housing problem, or something else about which I felt strongly, that, to me, was great. Coverage for me personally, or my face peering out at me from the paper over a controversial headline, put me off my stroke for days. On one occasion when I had drawn a lot of media comment over the telegram to the Pope, I went to Donegal for a week to avoid meeting people who might know about it.

Sometimes reportage could be provoked by the oddest outbursts. Har Byrne was a Labour man who in his final years as a politician rarely spoke in the Dáil. Once, he arrived and made a vitriolic attack on Gay Byrne which was so much out of the left field that it amounted to a marvellously sustained non sequiter. It was all over the papers the next day, even though it related not at all to the business of national importance which had been conducted in the Dáil before and after his spectacular arrival.

I was learning a touch of scepticism about the media. More seriously, I was learning a touch of cynicism about the Labour Party. Dissent. Isolation. Exclusion. It was an almost drearily repetitive pattern in the Labour Party. It had never been good at making pearls of the bits of grit under the Party skin, tending, instead, to extrude them, disregarding the value of variety or of having party thinking informed by those who differ on particular issues from the main stream of party minds. I had fought against so many expulsions that they melt into what seems to be a continuous battle in my memory.

One of the expulsions I most deeply regretted was that of Proinsias Mac Aonghusa. Proinsias had been involved in an internal party newsletter, which was both lively and vitriolic, quite often making personal attacks on the Party leadership, and it led to his expulsion. In the long run, he was expelled for what was essentially impertinence, because when the Party called on him to answer certain charges in connection with the newsletter, he challenged their right to do so, and as a result, out he went.

I was greatly disillusioned by this, and made an impassioned speech at the Rathmines branch of the Party saying that we must have room for dissent within the Party. It had no effect.

Then came a by-election in Wicklow in 1967. I involved myself in it, as was expected, except that in this instance I chose not to speak on platforms, but instead got lists of addresses and went from door to door on behalf of the candidate, just like any other canvasser.

Not long after the election, I was accused of not having played an active part in it. The then Chairman of the Party sent me a letter, saying that because of my "inactivity" the question would be brought before the Administrative Council, and implying that my nomination would not be ratified for the next General Election.

Recipe for a temporarily cynical Dr John O'Connell: steep him in poverty and social concern; pull him into a Party which, on the face of it, stands for eliminating the first and acting on the second; allow him to see that party concerning itself for the most part with internal squabbles, territorial and personality battles, taking action mostly to expel the brightest and best from within their own ranks and convince him that the crucial issues will never get their fair share of Party attention.

MacAonghusa and his wife, Catherine McGuinness, had made major contributions to the party. She had been personal secretary to Brendan Corish, had been an adviser and indefatigable worker and had written speeches for so many Labour TDs and here she was being treated so shabbily by the expulsion of her husband Proinsias.

I decided I had quite simply had enough, and that I was going to bail out. Leave public life. Stop right there. And this I did. I did not go to the Dáil. As far as the Party was concerned, I had fallen through a hole. And that must have lasted for nearly nine months. In one way, that sounds longer than in fact it was — Dáil holidays ordinarily take up something like five months of the year or more, so my absence was very much less than a year from the active political scene.

I had time, during that period, to think about politics, about myself and about where I was going. The problems which had brought me into the Labour Party seemed to me to have no prospect of being solved by that Party. The Labour Party was not, at that time, working hard enough at letting the people know what it stood for and where it could serve them. Documents were published and left to gather dust on shelves in Party HQ, and too much time was spent preaching to the converted.

The public was not aware of half of the Labour Party's policies, and this was not even a disquieting factor within a Party which had grown contented with relative failure, limited in expectation and in drive.

My absence was noted and the rumours flew. I was going to join Sinn Fein. (Oh, no, I was not.) I was going to join Fine Gael. (Oh, no, I was not.) Ironically, there was no suggestion at that point that I might join Fianna Fáil, but I had no intention of that either at that time.

The idea that I might join Fine Gael put my teeth on edge, because Fine Gael was seen by me as a totally right-wing party, opposed to any radical reforms in Irish politics. I was conscious of the fact that the Declan Costello policy document *Towards a Just Society,* which was an attempt to bring Fine Gael nearer to the centre, had been rejected out of hand by the Party.

So strong was the rumour of my joining Fine Gael, however, that Mary Maher from the *Irish Times* came to see me one evening to check on it. My gates were locked, and she jumped up on the taxi roof to get over them. It was made abundantly clear to her that whatever else I did, I would not join Fine Gael.

There were great problems for me in being out of politics. You cannot, in Ireland, get away from politics. It is almost easier to get away from drink. Every news bulletin on the radio, every discussion programme on television, every newspaper, everything reminded one of what was going on in the political arena.

There were, in addition, issues which burned me up and constantly tempted me back. During that period, I remember, there was a Language Freedom Movement meeting at the Mansion House and Sinn Fein tried to stop it taking place. The Language Freedom Movement was against compulsory Irish and for the right of parents to choose what languages their children would learn. That very nearly brought me back, because here were the Sinn Fein people who had got involved in the Griffith Barracks housing problem, and had spent their time prating about basic human rights, denying that most basic of human rights, free speech, to another group of people. I was so maddened, I wanted to go down there and confront them, but I decided that if I had left politics, I had left politics, so I sat and seethed at home.

But prolonged inactivity was like a death sentence for me. I needed to work. I felt if I was not working, I ceased to exist. So I cast about for a new challenge.

For some time, I had an idea at the back of my mind.

This was that there was a great need in Ireland for an independent medical newspaper.

I thought up a name — *Irish Medical Times* — got together an editorial board of opinion-makers within the profession, and explained that I planned to create a newspaper which would have a strong element of post graduate medicine in it, and also a strong medico-political side. It would provide doctors with a forum for discussion of current issues. I planned to pack it with good articles of a readable nature.

We launched the newspaper in January 1967, and doctors gave it a cautious welcome. How long was it likely to survive? This was the common reaction. I ran it initially with the aid of a sub-editor and a secretary.

I've always been conscious of the fact that *Irish Medical Times* must maintain a high standard of objective and unbiased reporting. So it was our established editorial policy from the outset never to become identified with narrow-minded party politics in our treatment of medico-political affairs. This is not to say that the newspaper is in any way inhibited from campaigning on important issues of the day. I have always, for example, advocated the right to family planning and *Irish Medical Times* has stood for the same thing since its inception.

I held that contraception was a matter of personal conscience, and that the State had no right to interfere. Further, I did not believe that the Church should ask the State to buttress its rules on the subject. By the time I had started the *Irish Medical Times*, I was a very different person to the daily Mass-going, unquestioning Catholic my parents had raised. Although still a Catholic, I was no longer unquestioning, and the authoritarian nature of the Church, and the insensitivity of some of its leaders to the major human problems of the day, had made me straightforwardly critical on occasion.

One of those occasions was during the Griffith Barracks episode, when at the height of the problem, the Archbishop of Dublin sent Monsignor Barrett down to the common room of the Barracks with a box of chocolates for the homeless people there. I went down to Westland Row to see the Monsignor, and we had a blazing row over that box of chocolates.

The pomp and the trappings of the Church also stuck in my throat. Even the fact that the Pope was carried on a dais annoyed me — the Originator of the whole thing walked, why couldn't his successor?

The arrival of Pope John XXIII at the Vatican did much to smooth my ruffled religious feathers, because I thought, here was a man who was everything a Pope should be, and I felt the organisation was moving in the right or rather the left direction. Pope John also hated the ritual of being carried, partly because it made him seasick, but he kept up the practice because he figured it allowed more people to see their Pontiff.

Of course, the *Irish Medical Times's* outspoken advocacy of family planning annoyed some doctors, and we had requests from them that they should be taken off our mailing list. Despite this, the *Irish Medical Times* has flourished and today, I believe it is an accepted part of Irish doctors' lives.

I was out of the Dáil, but busier than ever. In 1960, I had created MIMS, a publication designed to give doctors all the information they would need about new and existing drugs. Such a directory had not existed in Ireland or indeed elsewhere up to then, and doctors had to rely on cards sent out by the pharmaceutical firms, which were all very well in their way, but which you tended to shove in a drawer and lose when you most needed them. I once had the experience of having in my surgery a patient who was epileptic, and on whom I wished to try a new effective drug. No information, so, with the patient sitting there, I phoned the pharmaceutical company.

Oh yes, the girl said at the other end of the line, they'd be charmed to get the information for me, and their man would ring me back — next Tuesday!

I then decided that if nobody else would provide this necessary guide to the medicines doctors were prescribing every day, then I would. I was confident of the need for the publication, since, with the explosion in pharmaceuticals in the late fifties and early sixties, there were new substances on the market almost every week, and doctors needed some handy reference in which they could check for ingredients, contra-indications and so forth.

I developed the idea, and took it around to various firms producing medicaments, not introducing myself as a doctor, but simply as the editor of this proposed publication. In one firm, I was seen by the Managing Director and by the Marketing Manager. The Marketing Manager glanced over my proposal apathetically.

"Won't go," he said tiredly. "I know it won't."

"Why not?"

"Well, we KNOW doctors here, and I know from our experience, they won't use something like this."

"I think they will."

"They won't you know. Doctors don't like this sort of thing."

"Nonsense, and I AM a doctor."

I walked out of the meeting with full support from that particular company for a longer period than I had intended to request.

In due course, the first issue came out and started a success story that has run and run, at home and overseas. In Ireland four and a half thousand copies are printed, and MIMS is now an invaluable part of the doctor's life. It is also published in such countries as Australia, New Zealand, East and West Africa, the Middle and Far East and now America.

None of which surprised me, because I'd always been absorbed by the functions of editing. Even at primary school, I had edited a little magazine, as I had done in secondary school, and in the Labour Party, I produced *Labour News* for a long time. This was a monthly newspaper which was the equivalent of the British left-wing paper *Tribune,* the regular contributors being Proinsias MacAonghusa and Michael McInerney and Jim Downey of the *Irish Times.* I even sold it myself, hawking it in pubs, and Jim Kemmy supported it by having it circulated in the Limerick area.

Because of my self-inflicted political exile, I was out of touch with many of my political contacts, and relatively few of them stayed in touch. One exception was Michael McInerney, who had been a good friend and something of a mentor to me, lending me books and helping me to develop my political thinking.

At this time, 1968, he got in touch with me and asked me to have lunch in his flat with himself and Dr Conor Cruise O'Brien, who was then about to join the party, and who wanted some advice on how he might go about winning a seat in Dublin. I was very much in awe of O'Brien, seeing him as a political giant.

"Look," I said, "if you want to, you can run in my constituency, and I'll happily serve as your Director of Elections as I do not propose to contest the elections again."

He said he would think about it. It was an odd, three-cornered conversation, very formal between Conor Cruise O'Brien and myself, very informal between McInerney and me. I felt intuitively that O'Brien regarded me as a parochial politician, a grass-roots vote-getter, and I thought him a little stodgy.

I have always resented the assumption, indeed the myth that I am "just a vote-getter". I don't go to people's houses and plamas them. I have had stand-up rows on doorsteps, where people have said something with which I disagreed, rather than let the comment pass.

The other side to this is that I never make "political promises". I have never promised a political favour in my life. If people are not entitled to something, I will tell them so bluntly. If they are, I will never pretend that I got it for them out of influence, but will explain that this is their right, and that it is no more than that.

In the period after the meeting with Conor Cruise O'Brien (who never took me up on the offer of my support in my constituency) I became aware that things were happening in the Labour Party which were going to change it, probably for the better.

People like O'Brien, Justin Keating and David Thornley were coming into it, policy documents were being produced and disseminated, and there was a feeling that at last the Labour Party might be shaking off its ineffectual and old fashioned cap-and-muffler image and moving forward into the twentieth century, into a chance of sharing power on behalf of its adherents.

Almost against my will I began to be attracted back into the party, though I was very unsure of my welcome. In the event, when I did return, Frank Cluskey made a point of welcoming me back at the gates of Dáil Eireann. In due course, I was adopted as candidate for the General Election.

Not everybody was glad I had come back, of course. There were undoubtedly people who had hoped I would have the decency to stay in the wilderness since I had put myself there. Fortunately, they did not include my constituents, and I went to work for them twice as hard as before, in order to make up to them for my absence. Then I was back in the Dáil chamber, asking parliamentary questions by the hundred on the important issues as I saw them. I focused much of my energy on the housing crisis, which was made worse in 1969 by the shortage of Building Society funds and the high mortgage rates.

I raised the matter in the Dáil with a parliamentary question. When this failed to elicit a credible response, I attempted to pursue the matter further on the adjournment debate that evening and found the Minister short-tempered and intransigent. He refused to take any initiative and left the chamber without properly replying to the debate.

Then came the 1969 General Election. My constituency had been carved up and I now found I was being forced to stand in the same electoral area as the veteran Labour TD Sean Dunne, who was known as the King of Ballyfermot.

It was confidently predicted that I should be beaten as the political pundits anticipated only one Labour seat. The *Evening Press* in a political round-up of the constituency mentioned all the candidates except me.

I carried out a survey which indicated that Sean Dunne had a 69% popularity rating, and that I was a virtual unknown. However, I worked fiendishly in the campaign and in due course I was to beat Sean on first preference votes — the first time in Dublin that Labour won two seats in the one constituency.

Sean died six days later. It was a painful election result for that reason. Sean was a patient of mine for four years prior to the election, and we had been very good friends. I had a great admiration for him.

But because we were both thrown in together as competitors in this constituency, the rivalry clouded his thinking and he became suspicious of me — even as a doctor. At the time I was unaware of this, but when I visited him shortly before he died, he told me how he had been feeling.

"When I think of it, John," he said, "what we meant to each other was more important than politics."

I must admit, though, that, apart from the tragedy of Sean Dunne, that election had its amusing incidents, or at least its unexpectedly challenging moments. I knocked at one door in Ballyfermot and the man answering it said "Would you stop annoying me, I'm watching Sean Dunne on television." It was evens which of us would get to his TV screen quicker — him or me! Sean was brilliant on TV. Sean had an incredible facility for relating all the ills of Ireland to Ballyfermot, his own area, and he often said that he was so frequently on TV that he had a tan from the lights.

At another house, when I knocked, a harassed man poked his

head out.

"Listen," he said as I began to talk to him, "Buzz off, would you? I can't be listening to a politician, I'm much more concerned with my kid, who's just managed to stick a bead up her nose."

"Will you let me see if I can do anything about it? I am a doctor."

Doubtfully, he stood aside. I saw the child, removed the bead, applied an anti-biotic ointment I happened to have in my pocket.

"Well, if I wouldn't vote for you after that..." were his parting words.

At another time, I was going down a street when I heard blood-curdling screams coming from a house, and when I knocked, found a little nine year old girl had pulled a pot of boiling custard down all over herself. I whisked her straight off in a blanket to Dr Steevens Hospital, and had her admitted straight away. When I went back to tell the family what had happened, there was a welcoming party out for me.

The third incident in that odd series was towards the end of the campaign, when a motor-cyclist involved in a cavalcade through the streets came off his bike on a sharp corner. I was a few seconds away from him, and was able to give him immediate attention.

Before the end of the campaign, word got around that there was a Doctor O'Connell running and he was some kind of miracle man, appearing wherever a medic was called for.

This time, as I entered the Dáil, I did so feeling that now something was going to happen, now we had the energy and the intellect at our disposal, now we should be able to make the Labour Party into a force in the political life of Ireland. Now, we had men of charisma, of intellect, of charm. Men of high profile who attracted attention: Conor Cruise O'Brien. David Thornley. Justin Keating. Frank Cluskey. Michael O'Leary. They added up to a power potential the like of which the party had never seen.

Years later, when I saw television pictures of the American Challenger disaster, what it conjured up for me was what had happened to all that potential; one minute it was heading upward into the sunshine, all promise and excitement and drive, and the next minute it was breaking into smoky misdirection, worth watching mainly as an example of energy gone to waste.

Of the newcomers, I probably most admired Conor Cruise O'Brien, but did not know him.

It is a common misconception among members of the general public that if you are a member of the parliamentary party within a political party, you know everybody. Not true. Conor Cruise O'Brien was a distant figure. Distant, but civil. On one occasion I made an impassioned speech on contraception as part of a by-election campaign in Donegal. It brought down the wrath of the conservatives and of the Church — and the Labour candidate to this day is probably convinced I lost her deposit for her.

A few days later, passing by in the corridors of Leinster House, Cruise O'Brien noticed me and came over.

"You're a brave little man," he said. "A brave little man."

Faced with the daily exigencies of parliamentary performance, Cruise O'Brien was extremely nervous. He had to write out all of his supplementary questions; he adopted a careful formality and avoided the risks implicit in the spontaneity which Deputies like myself embraced. I was happy to bounce up and down and ask whatever supplementary question surged into my brain. The syntax and sentence structure were never as important to me as the purpose of the question and the possibility of achieving something.

Conor Cruise O'Brien would also twirl a pen incessantly between his fingers while he sat in the Chamber. The pen went round and round at such a pace you would swear there was a little motor attached to it. The tension that fuelled the speed of the pen never seemed to abate.

He is an orator, not a conversationalist. On one trip to the North — ironically, it was to welcome the British troops on their arrival, when it was believed that they would be a major factor in protecting the lives and property of Catholics there — although we were together for the duration, there was little conversation; he did talk to veteran Labour activist and broadcaster Jack Dowling who was also with us. I was later to find him a formidable opponent. I approached him on one occasion as he was Spokesman on the North and said that the violence in the North couldn't be allowed to go on, and that it was time that we all stopped patting ourselves on the back for not meeting with the IRA. Realism, I suggested, required that we talk to Sinn Fein.

At the time, he was amenable to my suggestion and said he would do so.

Later things were different. I have never understood why he wanted the whip removed from me, and the older I get, the madder I get about it. Bluntly, I now feel he had a damned cheek to seek to have me removed from the party for taking action designed to save lives and save the future of this country. It would be like suggesting that John Hume be removed from leadership of the SDLP because he met Sinn Fein in 1988 — ludicrous.

Conor Cruise O'Brien was a good statesman but was misplaced as Minister for Posts and Telegraphs, because I doubt if he really concerned himself in any broad positive developmental way with Posts and Telegraphs.

He is a man of formidable intellect, but that intellect is limited by its tendency to get stuck in grooves. One of those grooves was the issue of controlling terrorist access to media. Most important. But not important enough to distract from all of the other possibilities and imperatives within a Government department, and I felt he allowed it to do precisely that. In his newspaper writing since he left politics he has tended to channel his thinking into such predictable recurring lines that I feel I know precisely what he is going to say before I even read the piece.

He has been predicting civil war in the North for two decades. It has not happened as yet, but the prediction never loses its vehemence or its immediacy.

Similarly, he quite early on he developed an almost manic obsession with the personality of Charles J. Haughey. He relentlessly and personally pursued Haughey in the Dáil and everywhere else, to such an extent that the very persistence of his campaign allowed people to dismiss it as a personal vendetta.

If Conor Cruise O'Brien came into the Labour Party trailing clouds of internationalism, David Thornley came trailing clouds of glory from the world of television. He was the academic who had made it onto the prime time current affairs TV programme "7 Days", the precursor to "Today, Tonight". I had watched him often. Watched him interrogate people, including Jack Lynch, and had always been impressed by him. The round strong face. The unflinching directness of his eye on the camera or on the interviewee. The very individual, slightly English accent. The ruthless pointed questions and the visible impatience with waffle. The polished performer with the clean image.

I first met Thornley in the Labour rooms in the Dáil, shortly before a press conference to announce his entry into the Party. He did not know me, nor did he want to know or talk to anybody in the room. He was so patently eaten alive by nervousness that all of his energies went on reading and re-reading his speech notes. At the same time, he was using an electric shaver, going over and over his face as if he meant to erase it completely. It was startling to see an old television professional, veteran of so many tough on-screen confrontations, so fazed by the prospect of making a brief public appearance.

"What're they going to say to me?" he kept asking aloud. "What questions are they going to put?"

He was surrounded by a phalanx of Labour Party officers, some calling him "David" with something less than confidence in their voices, some "Doctoring" him, all of them agog with the sense of the honour he was doing the party by his presence.

In the later months, that phalanx gradually declined in numbers, but for some time, there was a great feeling of pride that the Labour Party had managed to attract someone of Thornley's fame and intellectual stature.

I saw relatively little of him, except in the House, and on one occasion, a few months after the election, he seemed unwell in the Dáil. It had been known for some time that he drank heavily. That day, it showed. I went over to him and asked if

101

there was any way I could help. I had to introduce myself first, because he scarcely knew me. He looked at me icily and, with frigid politeness, told me he needed nobody's help. I retreated.

I hoped at the time that what was happening was a short-term way of adjusting to changed circumstances. I knew the frustrations of the early months in the Dáil, only too well. If Dr Thornley was maddened by the slowness, the trivia, the lack of idealism he may have felt around him, then I had sympathy for him. Nor can it have been easy to switch over from being one of Ireland's best-known faces and most popular TV personalities to being a rank-and-file TD in an Opposition Party.

In one of the shifts within the Dáil, I ended up sharing a room with him. Sharing a room and initiating a friendship. He was disorganised, brilliant, always in a hurry, funny, open and childlike. I loved him, and within months of knowing him, saw clearly that this was a Greek tragedy already well under way.

I assumed, seeing him wilt under the stresses of politics, that he had found the disciplines of television easier. He had certainly come across as a figure of enormous energy and authority. Not so, however, as I learned from one of his colleagues and friends in RTE. Even as a highly successful TV performer, he had been devoured by stress.

The Dáil is a very small society of people who observe each other mercilessly. One TD made it his petty business to draw attention to Thornley's sleeping in the course of a Dáil debate, thus ensuring that a printed record noting his condition was available. By the end of that day, he was admitted to a nursing home, for treatment for alcoholism. By that time friends and opponents alike could see that Thornley's drinking was an illness, not an indulgence. He remained in the nursing home for some weeks and improved somewhat after his return to the Dáil.

His stories of his political life had a special interest. I had come to politics late. He had begun while in his teens. At sixteen he had fallen under the spell of Noel Browne and had worked for him in various campaigns. Noel Browne has always had this mystique for young people — they follow him, and always have followed him, as the children followed the Pied Piper. Especially the brightest and best — like David Thornley.

102

For David, as a young student, Browne was the great leader, the hero. He would have laid down his life for him, if Browne had asked it. Later, the relationship had its negative sides. David felt that Noel Browne never fully appreciated all that work that he, Thornley, had put in for him, never really thanked him, and he needed to be thanked, needed praise. He had a deep hunger for both.

As a talker, he was fascinating, second to none on the finer points of theoretical politics, although now, looking back, we seem to have discussed things other than politics for most of the time. I did know that he loathed practical politics, and had an almost physical revulsion against the personal contact involved in, say, holding constituency clinics. Real people with the real problems invaded him, made him uncomfortable, and he simply could not pretend that hail-fellow-well-met phoney friendship which comes so easily to so many politicians. Intellectually, he went along with it. Never in practice. He had the passion for the poor, but not the personal experience of poverty or of poor people, and so he would pick my brains for particular cases to illustrate issues he cared about, and I heard him time and again on public platforms quoting those cases.

"You know EVERYTHING, John," he would say, eyes twinkling, voice silky with derision.

It was the gap between theory and action that brought Thornley down.

He would promise that things would change, that he would work his constituency, develop every side of his career, and he would mean those promises, but somehow they were never fully realised. It was all the more tragic because he was not just a talented man, but a charming and pleasant one. I can remember parties in his house — quiet parties at which he would sing well and confidently. And I will never forget his simple courage on areas of his life which were open to ridicule.

He was, for instance, a fervent, and even curiously old-fashioned Catholic, with a great and unconcealed devotion to his religion.

"So I'm a Catholic, and I don't mind who knows it," he would say.

He had a photograph in the Labour Party rooms at the Dáil of himself meeting the Pope  an odd picture, snapped at the moment when the Pope's arms were at such an angle that he looked as if he was sparring with Thornley, the ex-boxer. Thornley carried rosary beads everywhere. Two members of the Party were expelled because they ridiculed him for those rosary beads.

He was methodical, too, making notes of what he had to do on a given day in a ring-bound notebook, and crossing the items off as they were done, or transferring them into the following day's list. The problem was that his priorities were not those of a politician, as illustrated by his pattern of answering letters. He would spend literally hours working on a witty response to a letter from a friend or a colleague, and leave no time for dealing with constituency letters.

As his months in the Dáil wore into years, I became more convinced than ever that politics was quite simply killing him. He had no oil on his political feathers. He could be too easily hurt. I said this publicly, and deeply offended his wife by so doing. I thought that if he got out of politics and back into university life where he was respected and would be valuable, then there was a chance that his illness might be halted and that he might live to be old, whereas it was evident that as a politician, he would not. I felt that his life had to be more important than the Labour Party, more important than politics. But he could not let go. When I talked to him, trying to persuade him to give up and go out of active politics, he would become suspicious.

"Come on John," he would say. "Who's prompting you to do this?"

The public, of course, seeing Thornley episodically on TV, was conscious of little of what was happening to him. Physically, of course, there were changes, more shocking to people who saw him infrequently. In a matter of a few years, he changed almost completely, and was acutely conscious of it. The problem was, of course, that when the public DID hear about him, it was often in contexts which did him damage and which created an image which had nothing to do with the reality. To this day, people think of him as a rabid Republican. Yet in the early years of the Northern troubles, I met him in South Anne Street one day and told him that members of the Parliamentary Labour Party were going to the North.

"I'm not very happy about the friends the Party is making up there," he said. "Some of my best friends are Unionists".

He appeared at an IRA demonstration, on the platform, to the dismay of his friends and to the boos of the IRA supporters. The air was thick with cries of:

"Labour Party traitors off the platform, please!"

It was easy for those who wanted to, to make the simplistic judgement that he was a Provo sympathiser, whereas the reality of it was that he felt strongly, at all times, about basic civil rights, including, in the case of the IRA demonstration, the right to free speech. I felt the Labour Party members were cruel to him on this episode. They met to expel him, and I pleaded for him, conscious that he was pacing the corridor outside, sick with worry, because he needed to be a member of the Party. At this time particularly, the Party should have been supportive, particularly since, if we're to talk politics rather than human considerations, they had nothing to lose.

Carefully analysed, it was obvious to anyone with a grain of political sense that Thornley was such an individualist, and seen as such by the general public, that whatever he did was credited to him, not to the Labour Party, so there was no reflection on the Party, nothing to get so worked up about.

At a Parliamentary Labour Party meeting, I argued that he had been isolated by the Party at a time when he needed help most.

"He knew my telephone number," Brendan Corish said.

"Who knows your telephone number?" I demanded. "Since we've been in power, you've been ex-directory. My God, I don't know your telephone number, how do you expect David Thornley to?"

I was strongly supported in my efforts to stave off Thornley's expulsion by Michael D. Higgins from Galway. Michael, like myself, believed that the party should get on with its work rather than play the "who shall we expel today?" game, and he also believed that David, at that time, needed a crutch and the crutch was the Labour Party. Thornley was struggling so hard then, doing his level best. We failed, and he was expelled.

I was the first out into the corridor to tell him. He was desperately shaken, on the verge of tears, just wanting to find some corner and hide in it, and he was hell-bent on shaking off the media-men eager to talk with him now the news was filtering out.

"Wait, David," I said, "You must talk to them—"

"I won't. I can't."

"Listen to me. If you talk now, explain your case, you can get tremendous public sympathy. The public should know why you did what you did. You can't — it'd be wrong to give them the impression that you support illegal organisations. You know that. Look, trust me. Be guided by me — talk to them."

After a long moment he nodded.

"All right. I'll do it, I'll talk to them."

He was superb in those interviews, and came out completely on top. The newspaper columns were full of him and how impressive he had been. I am convinced that if there had been a general election coming up at that time, he'd have topped the poll. But there it was. He was, for the moment, out of the Party, not under the whip anymore, although it made little difference. He voted consistently with the party — more consistently than John O'Connell, who, on occasion, abstained on this issue or that, where Thornley never did. After about a year, he was accepted back. There had been tremendous if unexpressed sympathy for him during his period of exile, although I suspect that few understood how greatly that exile made him suffer.

His illness progressed inexorably, and he talked to his close friends of his death wish, his conviction that he would die young. Once, in the Dáil, he was taken ill so badly that it was a miracle he survived, and I remember him lying on a couch in the corridor, waiting for the ambulance to come.

Luke Belton, the Fine Gael TD was there, I recall, and Thornley, who was at his most gallant and courteous when he was sickest, smiled at him and murmured, "This is one by-election coming up I shan't be called on to take an active part in." Meaning, of course, the by-election caused by his own death. However he recovered, and decided unshakably that he would run for the '77 election. I told him it would kill him, that there was no good purpose to be served by running.

"If you go now David, gracefully, you're winning," I said, so many times. "People will always say you could have won. You can get out, lose nothing."

"Let me go forward this once," he said, almost to himself, "and I'll never do it again."

I think he felt that he could just make it, just retain his seat. But the campaign drained him completely. The glamour of so few years before was no longer there. He was tired, sick, and the slow-motion progress to inevitable defeat was agonising. I hadn't helped in this progress by being instrumental in having him nominated to the European Parliament. The air-commuting, with its periods of sitting in airports, had done nothing but complicate his illness. Now, at the end of it, he lost his Dáil seat. Even then, he had the lively ability to poke fun at himself.

"I become more like Buddha every day," he said, smiling. "So I shall first take a holiday in Kilkenny, and then devote some time to the contemplation of my navel."

A matter of weeks afterwards, he was dying. I remember thinking what a tragedy it was, not for him, because for him the sickness and pain were over, but for the rest of us and particularly for his family. He could have been such a tremendous influence, such a powerful force. The brilliance in theoretical politics was there, the wit, the charm. But as a practical politician, he was a student to the end, and a mediocre student. I'm not sure that he would be sorry to have that comment made about him . . .

Michael O'Leary, by contrast, was a fast learner, a born survivor. A pragmatic socialist, O'Leary is a man with wit and the capacity to make people laugh. I remember at some point in the seventies, he and Noel Browne were together on some kind of Labour Party fact-finding mission to the North and all stayed in the house of a Labour man in Newry. Because Noel Browne was viewed as being a little bit delicate, physically, the main bedroom was given up to him, and all the others — five of them, including O'Leary mucked in together in the other room. O'Leary made much of the inroads this communal living had made on his night's sleep.

"It was like sleeping with a lot of Saracen tanks, the snoring was so bad," he claimed.

O'Leary had a rare gift of mimicry. He could do a take-off on anybody, and although I never saw him imitate me, I would have no doubt that he'd do it easily, instinctively, and well enough to make my skin crawl.

Now, we had strength in the Labour Party. Strength, public credibility, and a potential partner in Government with some semblance of social conscience.

Declan Costello's thinking had attracted a lot of young people into Fine Gael, and kicked a new spirit of social justice into that party. I admired him greatly. Not only that, but I had tried to persuade him to go up for the by-election in my area, to fill the vacancy created by the death of Labour TD Sean Dunne. I was so enthusiastic about this that not only did I go to him and see him on a daily basis but I also saw his father, John A. Costello, a former Taoiseach. I was just so anxious that he become involved, so concerned that a mind of such generosity and vision be allowed to shape the future of this country. It was one of the many times when I could see no party political angles — if this man thought this way, Ireland needed him, even if I was surprised to find him in Fine Gael as opposed to the Labour Party.

When he retired from the scene I thought it was wrong. I went to see him and told him so, but he said he could not be reconciled with Liam Cosgrave.

I also went to see Garret FitzGerald. At that time I told him I thought the *Just Society* document was great and that they could not afford to lose a resource like Declan Costello and that they should persuade him to come back into politics. Declan did come back into politics in 1973 as a Fine Gael TD for Ballyfermot, became Attorney General in the Coalition

Government but appeared not too enamoured of the political scene. He withdrew from politics in 1977.

The Labour Party had campaigned actively against our entry into the EEC, though some in the Parliamentary Party were half-hearted in support of Labour's stand, particularly Conor Cruise O'Brien, who believed we should not oppose EEC entry. In the event the Irish people by an overwhelming majority decided we should join, and Labour was left to nurse its bruises.

I became very impatient with Labour and its complacent attitude to politics and said as much at a Labour Party dinner in Seamus Pattison's constituency in Kilkenny in October 1971. My criticism of the leadership was widely reported, and Brendan Corish took it as a personal slight. The matter was raised at the next meeting of the Administrative Council of the party. At this time Roddy Connolly, son of the famous 1916 leader James Connolly, was Chairman of the Labour Party, and he was delegated to see me and seek an explanation and apology for what I had said in my speech. He came to my office in Merchant's Quay, but by the time he climbed the stairs to my second floor office he was markedly breathless, so much so that he was unable to speak except with difficulty. I immediately got my medical bag and checked him over. I then gave him some tablets and told him to take them three times daily.

By the time my clinical examination was completed Roddy had forgotten the real purpose of his visit to me, which was to seek an explanation and apology. And when he returned to Labour Party headquarters and was asked what did O'Connell say, Roddy Connolly promptly replied, "he said I was to take these tablets three times a day."

I felt the Labour Party was getting nowhere so I initiated the possibility of Coalition and made the first speech on it. There were harsh memories among older TDs of an earlier Coalition, but I was too new to politics to remember that, and so I was not bogged down by precedent. It was all future tense and possibilities. Moves began to get underway. I was pushing hard, because I felt there was no point in knocking at doors, as a Labour Party member, and saying to an old age pensioner "don't you worry missus — when we're in power in 30 years time you'll be living in the lap of luxury".

Having made the initial speech, I then persuaded Brendan Corish to come out three weeks later to Inchicore to make a similar speech. He communicated with Liam Cosgrave in advance and told him he was going to make a statement calling for some kind of pact on the transfer of preferences. This was the first time in sixteen years that there was the possibility of an alternative government. Up to this time Corish as Leader of the Labour Party had publicly proclaimed his opposition to any form of coalition.

Liam Cosgrave and he had agreed that Cosgrave as leader of Fine Gael would reply in a positive way that same night. Suddenly, it was up and running, and I was pushing hard to keep the momentum going. Speeches anywhere and everywhere. Phone calls. Accosting people in Leinster House corridors. John Bruton of Fine Gael thought I was pushing it so hard it might be counter-productive. I met John and he said to me that I should slow down. But there's a tide in the affairs of men, and I was determined to take this one at the flood. Labour seemed to be invigorated by the prospect. There were people — Noel Browne was one of them — who did not favour it. Noel was totally opposed to it and I remember there was a conference, a lot of problems raised and a lot of fury vented, but the Labour Party survived. Coalition seemed to promise an awful lot for the party. It seemed to me that the men and women we had were too good to waste in permanent opposition.

Permanent opposition was an enviable position of chronic excusable failure. Nothing could be achieved, therefore you couldn't be judged or punished for failure to achieve. You had the luxury of safe condemnation of all of the other players, knowing that you would never be called onto the field yourself. It turned idealists into phrase-making poseurs.

I also had doubts about any single party continuing in Government after sixteen years rule. Fresh thinking and a different approach were, I believed, overdue.

The public suddenly became conscious of the fact that at last there might be an alternative to the sixteen year Fianna Fáil rule and this manifested itself in two by-election defeats for Jack

Lynch in late 1972. But perhaps what hastened the onset of a General Election was the planting of the bombs in Dublin on 1 December 1972, which caused great public fear. At the time Fianna Fáil was endeavouring to push through the Dáil the Offences Against the State (Amendment) Bill 1972, which was being vigorously opposed by Fine Gael's Paddy Cooney and Labour's Conor Cruise O'Brien. Liam Cosgrave was understood to be very unhappy with Fine Gael's stand against the Bill but he was overruled by the liberal wing of the Party led by FitzGerald and Cooney. At that point Cosgrave's position as leader of Fine Gael was becoming very precarious. But just before the Bill was being put to a vote news suddenly broke in Leinster House that a number of bombs had gone off in the city centre. Deputies were beginning to have second thoughts on the Government's Bill, and Cosgrave took advantage of the confusion and uncertainty within Fine Gael and proposed that Fine Gael withdraw its opposition to the Bill. This was later agreed and Cooney then had to swallow his pride and stand up in the House and say:

> I beg leave of the Chair and the House to intervene in the debate at this stage in my position as proposer of this reasoned amendment on behalf of the Fine Gael Party. I should like to remind the House that our amendment was designed to show opposition to the Bill as drafted while, at the same time, indicating that we support all reasonable measures to enforce law and order. Tragic events have overtaken Parliament and conscious, and indeed anxious, about the fact that our amendment, if supported by those Members of the House known as the dissidents and now revealed as fellow-travellers of the IRA might have the effect of plunging the country into the turmoil of a political crisis when, above all, in view of recent events stability is required, we have decided to put nation before party and accordingly we withdraw our amendment, but in no way conceding that a Bill of such a repressive nature as this Bill should be of more than temporary duration and subject to mature consideration later.

Garret FitzGerald was furious at his party's volte-face.

The bombing had a devastating effect on Brendan Corish who felt that Labour's opposition to the Fianna Fáil Bill must be cast aside in the light of the changed circumstances caused by the bombs, especially as it was widely believed at that moment that it was the IRA who had planted the bombs.

"Brendan," I said, "if we do an about turn now after the stand we took against the Bill, we'll lose all *credibility* as a Party. We've no alternative but to vote against it".

I was supported by Michael O'Leary, and Brendan Halligan, who, though not a TD at that time, was Corish's closest adviser and confidant. Corish very reluctantly consented to our voting against the Bill. Leinster House that night was rife with rumours that Jack Lynch was about to call an election but the timing was most inappropriate as it would have meant polling day being set for Christmas Eve with the count taking place on St Stephen's Day.

Had Jack Lynch yielded to the temptation to call the election the night of the bombing, I firmly believe he would have won a massive majority, as his television appearance that night reassuring a frightened public won him overwhelming support. I felt he missed a great opportunity, for when he did call the election six weeks later the issues had changed. The public's priorities were now prices and the economy, not law and order, and the combined opposition of Fine Gael and Labour exploited these issues for all they were worth.

I enjoyed that election campaign, enjoyed the sensation of forward motion, the campaign motto, "We've got to get them *out*," even though I had found myself earnestly trying to convince a young mother with two children of the truth of that motto, only to be rocked back on my heels when she stopped me in my talk and said gently, "Would you ever tell me who's *in*?"

It was an exciting election result in many ways; firstly because the decision to form a National Coalition brought the desired effect in vote transfers between Fine Gael and Labour, a strategy which neutralised the actual percentage vote increase which Fianna Fáil achieved in the election. It was also exciting because we were seeing the first change of Government in sixteen years.

It was an election of shocks and surprises — shock at the defeat of such an important Fianna Fáil Minister as Brian

Lenihan in Longford, surprise at the many cliff-hangers that finally went the Coalition's way. In eight constituencies the last seat was won by less than 600 votes, and Labour's own candidate, John Ryan, scraped home in North Tipperary by the remarkably narrow margin of 143 votes. In contrast, Labour's candidate Ruairi Quinn in Dublin South East failed by as little as 39 votes in the final count. My own election result was even better than I had hoped for with almost 10,000 first preference votes; in percentage vote terms I came second in the country only to Jack Lynch himself.

Jack Lynch's appearance on television with a tear in his eye as he conceded defeat and commiserated with his colleague Brian Lenihan was a very moving scene, and I felt that if at that moment the public had a second chance, it might have had second thoughts. Indeed the following morning, this was confirmed to me by the icy-cold reception I received from my constituents when I went to thank them for my vote. The general reaction to the Coalition victory was unenthusiastic to say the least.

"We'll just wait and see." It was then that I became consciously aware of just how fragile was the public acceptance of the National Coalition.

With Labour winning 19 seats as against Fine Gael's 54, it was understood that at least five of the ministries would go to our party. I had a fair expectation that I might gain one of those ministries, since Michael O'Leary had come up to my selection conference three weeks earlier and said to all the delegates there, "In three weeks time John O'Connell will be Minister for Health." Michael O'Leary was very close to Brendan Corish, so it was a fair assumption that it was a prediction that might be delivered on. The newspapers certainly made that assumption and built it into their coverage during the interim days. Their expectation buttressed my own, and so it was a great disappointment to me at the time. A very, very great disappointment to me when it did not happen, because I had all sorts of plans for health. They came to nought at the time.

At the first Parliamentary Labour Party meeting following

113

the election, Corish walked in and announced that the first item on the agenda was the election of the Party leader. A usual procedure, this, after every general election. The issue was never in doubt. It was understood that his re-election would be just a formality — but his attitude was somewhat strange.

"I want to make it absolutely clear," he began, "right here and now that I will only accept the leadership on condition that I, and I alone, have the final say in the selection of Labour Ministers".

This was a bombshell, and from what I understood, was against all established procedure, but he had a gun to our heads, and stunned consent greeted him. Consent backed by confusion, since a number of rural TDs had not got to the meeting, because they had been told that no issues of any great importance would be discussed at that meeting. I felt a number of questions had to be considered first, but it was like being mowed down by a train — the names of the five Ministers were announced, Corish, Cruise O'Brien, Keating, O'Leary and Tully, and Corish walked out without another word.

There was a feeling of bewilderment and disquietude among the members of the party. This was so unlike the Corish we all knew — he was never the man to be dogmatic on any issue. In fact the opposite might be nearer the truth.

The first day of the new Dáil with the National Coalition in power was as exciting as was the election result. Both Fine Gael and Labour deputies were to sit in the opposition benches until Liam Cosgrave's election as the new Taoiseach. I found myself sitting next to Paddy Cooney, the Fine Gael TD.

"Paddy, were you not made a Minister?" I asked.

"No, John, I wasn't," he replied, rather disconsolately, I thought.

"Oh, I'm sorry to hear that, you deserved to be," I replied.

Just at that moment Liam Cosgrave beckoned him, and he was in, as Minister for Justice. I was as delighted for him as I was disappointed for myself. It always puzzled me as to why Cosgrave should leave until the last minute the decision as to who should be Minister for Justice, and I remember thinking, given Cooney's reputation at that time as a liberal, that perhaps,

114

while Cooney might hold the portfolio, Cosgrave might be the real Minister for Justice.

For me, being a backbencher in that particular Coalition was hell, because I was constantly taking the rap, at constituency level and in public, for what our Ministers were doing or not doing, and I had no control whatsoever over either. I was forced to accept compromises which stuck in my throat and gave me moral indigestion. I took a stand on particular issues — such as the question of repressive legislation, and was humiliated when forced to withdraw my amendments.

I was totally isolated. I remember going to Brendan Corish to know what kind of a role I could play as a backbencher and he very nicely sidestepped the issue.

"I've only got three minutes to talk to you," he said, and ended up telling me that he now had five phones and showed me how they worked and all the rest. That was the extent of our conversation — telling me about the phones.

"See that phone there — now that goes direct to..." That was it.

I did manage to mention about the unavailability of a booklet on eligibility for Social Welfare benefits.

Many copies of the booklet were in his office.

"Brendan they shouldn't be up here — the people should have them — let people know what they're entitled to," I said, never having seen these books in use by the people who should have been able to use them.

"Do you know how much they cost? 35p each," he replied.

How do you talk to a man who would say that?

One of the things I demanded was that the old age pension which workers had provided for in their weekly contributions be not liable to income tax, but I was ordered to withdraw my amendment by the Labour Party an order made more infuriating by the fact that Jack Lynch, then leader of the Opposition, told me his party would support me. Of course, at that time, there was the vague promise that Richie Ryan, Minister for Finance, would consider it in his next budget — a vague, and, as it turned out, meaningless sop to me.

There had been much talk of how Fianna Fáil after sixteen

years in office had become arrogant. But it became increasingly obvious that the Coalition had become arrogant within 16 months. And, at a more practical level, I felt that the work being done was not sufficiently energetic. After so many years in Opposition, I believed that the lights should never have gone out in the Ministers' offices. I said so, and was clipped by various people, including Justin Keating, the Coalition's Minister for Industry and Commerce who told me bluntly to toe the line or else.

What I found most interesting, viewing the Coalition from a unique standpoint as the inside outsider, was that the people of whom most had been expected were, in Government, disappointing — and those of whom little had been expected were, occasionally, very fine as Ministers.

Brendan Corish had been expected to be a compassionate and far-sighted Minister for Health and Social Welfare. In fact, I suspect he scarcely came to grips with the Department of Health before he was out of it — a common failing with Coalition Ministers, who seemed to be very much at the mercy of their senior civil servants.

I remember one instance where I came into conflict with Mr Corish. It was a simple individual case which showed where any Government Minister could, without major cost to the exchequer, have made a compassionate gesture simply by amending the regulations slightly. What happened was that a woman in my constituency who had cancer of the gullet was unable to swallow solid food and could only swallow Complan, a semi-liquid food.

She had a medical card, and I was requesting that the Complan be made available to her on the medical card, which at that time was not possible, because technically, Complan was not a medicine, and so did not come under the scheme. But many patients with digestive disorders needed to have Complan prescribed. I went to see Brendan Corish, who as Minister for Health was responsible, I outlined the problem and he was understanding. He would see what could be done. I went to him again. He had forgotten, but not to worry, he would see what could be done. I went to him a third time. This occasion, he was brusque in refusal.

"Well, no, that can't be done."

"Well, Brendan, I'm going to put down a parliamentary question to you about it."

"You do what you like."

I put down my question and got an unsatisfactory answer, and so requested permission to raise the matter on the Adjournment. Fought it through, getting nowhere, more maddened than ever by a message which arrived in the course of the afternoon. At last I concluded, sick at heart.

"It doesn't matter now anyway," I said bitterly. "She's dead".

Of the five Labour Ministers in the Coalition Government the performance I found surprisingly positive was that of Jim Tully, Minister for Local Government, in spite of a widespread feeling in the Party that he was so right wing he had no place in a proper Labour Party.

He was, they said, no real socialist, yet he surprised everybody by being one of our most active Ministers, pushing through a housing programme the like of which we had not seen in years. He was also accessible. I talked to him, praising the housing developments, but complaining that the growth in living places was not evenly spread. Dublin was not doing well, I said. Nonsense, he said, quoting a figure. I quoted another — Dublin Corporation that year had built only 405 extra houses.

"Not true", he said.

"Check your facts, Jimmy," I replied. "You'll find I'm right".

He did. And proved himself a good Minister and a good man, in my view, by bouncing right back to me with a positive response, rather than a well-thought out defence.

"I'm making ten million more pounds available for housing in Dublin," he told me.

He impressed me all during the Coalition as a pragmatic Socialist, not bound up in theory, but conscious of people's needs and responding to them in an honest practical way.

In May 1976 Fianna Fail TD Noel Lemass died, which meant a by-election in my constituency. It was a particularly significant by-election, as it was the first test in Dublin of public reaction to the Coalition Government.

At this particular time my relationship with the party hierarchy was at a very low ebb, and the local Labour organisation was not happy at the prospect of winning the seat for the Coalition. They were very disillusioned with the Coalition's performance and particularly with Labour's participation in it.

It was decided to ask Noel Browne to stand but when I mentioned this at a Parliamentary Party meeting all hell broke loose.

"Noel Browne — never, " they chorused.

I suddenly had visions of a repetition of the 1970 by-election fiasco in Dublin South-West which resulted in Labour losing a safe seat. In the event Noel Browne refused the offer, saying that he couldn't in conscience stand as it would mean endorsing Cosgrave and his policies. On the local level we were in a dilemma. The political correspondents were saying I held the key to this election, that whoever I put forward would win. I was far from confident. And I knew that I would get the blame if Labour lost. Why should I take on this responsibility? Hasty consultations with the local Labour organisation.

"Why not propose the darlin' of the Labour leadership?" said Paddy Vickers, our constituency chairman.

"Indeed why not?" said our constituency secretary, Paddy McNamara.

"I think that's a great idea and let them go out and win it for him."

Selection conference arranged at which Jim Tully was to preside. Slight hassle. And then in his absence, and without his knowledge or consent, Brendan Halligan, General Secretary of the Labour Party, was proposed, seconded and selected as Labour's candidate.

When the news became public, the Labour hierarchy was aghast.

Just what trickery was O'Connell up to, they wanted to know. But it was no trickery. With the odds so much against the Coalition Government in Dublin South West — inflation

118

running at 18% and a local unemployment level of 23% — the Labour organisation believed that it would take a nationally known figure to win it. However while Brendan Halligan may have been General Secretary of the Labour Party, and an economist of some repute, who made frequent TV appearances on RTE political programmes, to the people of Dublin South-West he was a total stranger, as they generally watched BBC and ITV. This was brought home very forcefully to me by our Director of Canvassing, who declared that to win the seat, it would mean my bringing Halligan personally to virtually every door in the constituency.

In the event we won the seat. But victory was due not to the Labour Ministers who, with the notable exception of Conor Cruise O'Brien, made infrequent appearances in the constituency, but to the combined efforts and dedication of the local organisation and Labour branch members from all over the country.

Michael O'Leary, the Coalition Government's Minister for Labour was later to say that if they had lost that by-election, they would have won the General Election because socks would have been pulled up — and pulled up in time.

As it was, the Coalition lost the General Election one year later and it came as no surprise to me. I had been conscious of the change in public attitude even before the campaign began. It wasn't just a case of "Get them out," it was a case of "How SOON can we get them out?"

Cosgrave's total misreading of the election issues and his failure to offer any positive alternative to the alluring promises in the Fianna Fail Manifesto, set the seal on the Coalition's defeat. When the Fianna Fail manifesto was published it was confidently expected that the Coalition would respond with an attractive alternative. Indeed, Jim Tully, who as a senior Minister must have been privy to the Government's electoral strategy, was heard to say: "We're going to come out with a document that'll make them sick!".

The document which was "to make Fianna Fail sick," of course, never appeared and six months later I asked him why.

"Because the Department of Finance wouldn't let Richie

Ryan publish it, that's why."

"I've more contempt now than ever, hearing that the civil servants ran the Government." I said.

In my constituency, I was very lucky to maintain the vote I achieved in 1973 as there was a 7% swing against the Coalition in Dublin, and unemployment was rife in my area.

Directly after the Coalition defeat, the question of leadership of the Labour Party came up and was settled, with, I thought, indecent haste. Certain elements in the Party who had persuaded Brendan Corish to stay on for so long, now could not wait to get rid of him. The vote took place so soon that Sean Treacy, the Labour T.D. for Tipperary South couldn't vote because he was technically still the Ceann Comhairle. I felt it was undemocratic.

I had indicated in advance to Frank Cluskey, one of the two candidates, that I was sorry but I couldn't support him, as I had already committed my support to Michael O'Leary. This was a difficult situation for me, as both he and Michael O'Leary were friends of mine. However, I had given a commitment to O'Leary, and honoured that commitment even after a tie vote.

On the opening day of the 22nd Dáil, with a Fianna Fáil Government about to take over, I was to witness a very dispirited group of Coalition Ministers having lunch in the special dining room reserved for the Cabinet. I felt strangely sorry for them, and tried to introduce a note of levity with a flippant remark.

"This looks more like the Last Supper," I offered.

Frozen unsmiling silence was the response. As it was the response to the cruel parliamentary ritual of sitting in the Cabinet benches in the chamber until the Dáil went through the formality of electing the new Taoiseach Jack Lynch, and then having to transfer to the Opposition benches.

As I watched, I saw 15 men, who had come into Government four and a half years previously to change the social realities and political life of the country — and had failed.

Fianna Fáil's victory was an overwhelming one, nowhere more evident than on the opening day of the Dáil when their 84 deputies literally overflowed on to the Labour benches, and I

120

found sitting beside me Fianna Fáil's new Deputy for Co Louth, Eddie Filgate. In a sense, this continued a trend which had begun when Fianna Fáil were in opposition and I had got to know a great many of them as individuals, having set up a medical room in Leinster House where some of them came as patients, showing none of the arrogance which was all too evident when they were in Government.

Now, the Labour Party was out of Government, and back in the familiar role as Opposition with Frank Cluskey as Leader. And I was heading for trouble, because of the way I saw Opposition and the different way my party saw it. I became convinced that the role of an Opposition Party was not merely to oppose in a ritualistic sense. If a Government introduced good, reforming legislation, then it was, as I saw it, the duty of an Opposition to give credit, not to seek to see something bad in every single thing a Government did. So I would praise Ministers for what they had done, even send letters of congratulations on particular pieces of legislation. By the same token, I felt Governments had a duty to give greater opportunity to the Opposition to initiate legislation. They should not reject something simply because it emanated from the Opposition. If this positive approach were to be taken, I believed, then we'd be on our way to growing up in the Dáil, getting rid of old stereotyped political positions, and allowing our minds to clear themselves of old, narrow thinking.

We had a newly sophisticated public who wanted to see changes and were not interested in the old-style pantomime posturing. Of course, by taking this stance, I immediately alienated some friends in the Party, but I couldn't continue to make the pretence of attacking moves of which I approved just for the sake of party allegiance or friendship.

The biggest problem facing any politician who goes in to the Dáil with the sort of aims which motivated me, is the softening effect of time spent in the place. The danger is that all your sharp edges will be worn down, and you will be swallowed up in what I call the "Kildare Street Club."

You need enough time to get to know the procedures and the methods of working, but not too much time. Not enough time to

121

become a political empty suit; a likeable, impotent fixture, known to all and without an uncompromised principle left in him or any heat left in his angers.

That is one of the reasons I have such unwavering regard for Labour TD Michael D. Higgins. I think he is a great person, always way ahead of the party in his thinking. A most articulate person. But most of all, a man who after years in politics, still feels passionately about issues.

I have seen him over the years since he first joined the Labour Party, and today, I see him as the soul of the party. He and Emmet Stagg are men who are in touch with the real problems on the ground and feel strongly about issues. In this country, we are very good at admiring and simultaneously disregarding the Noel Brownes, the Michael D. Higgins and the Emmet Staggs of the political world. It makes us feel broadminded to admire them and practical to dismiss them.

Re-drawing of constituency boundaries in 1980 caused more friction. Frank Cluskey was leader of the Labour Party and it so happened thatthe redrawing of the constituencies  meant that Frank and I would be in the same constituency.

I was regarded at that time as a very good vote getter; I topped the poll at all times, and Frank was a person who always scraped in at the end. His prestige was at stake here, and I could understand that but what was wrong was that Frank would not assume good in other people. I admired him, found his grasp of *realpolitik* astute and amusing, wanted him to succeed. Had Frank said to me, "I want you to go to East Mayo," I would gladly have gone. Instead, he cut me off at the pass.

When we came to the convention or selection conference, in January 1981, I saw all his people move in. I saw him come in and ignore me as if I was not there. I saw the cards were stacked. I got votes from my own branch but from none of the others and so I failed to get the Party's nomination.. I stood up and congratulated Frank on his selection. A person selected instead of me was a man named Joe Connolly.

The following morning I received a phone call from Frank and he asked me to go in to see him. In the  newspapers that morning it said that Joe Connolly would not be going forward so I would now be next in line.

"I'm awfully sorry I didn't say hello to you last night," he said. I didn't pursue it,

"Now Frank, with Joe Connolly withdrawing I suppose I can now be added to the ticket."

"Oh no. I've a good man for that. He's a local councillor. Andy. He's very good."

"But Frank, last time out he only got 238 votes!"

"It doesn't matter. He's the man."

End of story. Bottom line. Dismissal.

I went on television and expressed annoyance and disappointment at not being selected. This was 1981. I had been part of the Labour party in the Dáil since 1965.

I was a redundant gadfly.

# Chapter 6

# Wilson, the North and the IRA

The sixties wore on into the seventies and the violence in the North, exacerbated rather than controlled by the imposition of internment, showed signs of developing into a chronic problem. It was a problem I believed had to be solved, so I found ways to talk to everybody who might listen, who might influence, who might change things. This was the time when I first got to know Ian Paisley. Later, as a Member of the European Parliament, I got to know him even better and to count him and his wife Eileen as good friends, especially this great blustering physical invasion, this man who displaces air simply by entering a room. By 1972 I was convinced that many of the earlier options for peace in the North had foundered because of the way Paisley had been handled. Too many of those involved wilfully refused to recognise him as a figure of power and influence. They preferred to dismiss him as a demagogue and to parody him as an almost comical figure.

In the process, they painted him into a political corner, narrowing the choices open to a powerful and important force in Northern Ireland affairs.

Through me, Paisley came close to meeting Charles Haughey. There were discussions and we arranged it a few times but it just fell through. But Ian Paisley did ask me if Charles Haughey would insert into his first Ard Fheis speech as Taoiseach and leader of the party a section indicating that the interests of the Unionists were as much the Taoiseach's concern as were those of the Catholic minority in Northern Ireland. Mr.

Haughey did include that in his speech in March, 1980.

The Irish Constitution caused constant problems to Paisley's political aide, Jim Allister.

"How can you expect us to talk to you on equal terms while Articles Two and Three of the Constitution are there. How can you?" Jim Allister asked me one night over dinner. But Ian Paisley said to him "Look Jim, you've got to be realistic, you can't expect them to remove Articles Two and Three from the Constitution like that." Ian Paisley putting my arguments for me...

Paisley would tell me stories about how, before he ever went to a Government office to sort out a constituent's problem, he would first make his impending presence felt.

"I phone up and tell them I'll be down in twenty minutes and then I have them wait twenty minutes and that's a psychological thing," he said in his broad Northern accent..

It sounded to me like a fairly good-humoured and highly effective form of intimidation, but I suspected that its successful use required the Paisley name and the Paisley physical stature.

Paisley would tell me, too, about his time in prison and about the horrible porridge concoction which they called "donkey's vomit." He never forgot the face of the policeman who had actually arrested him, and years later he would create situations in which the unfortunate officer had to salute him. Just for the hell of it. But behind all the hell and damnation and demonic demagoguery is a kind person. He showed this great concern for his wife Eileen when her father died. She was very depressed and he was so caring.

So, at the time I was talking with Paisley, I was also talking frequently with the SDLP. I was talking with Sinn Féin. Eventually I felt it was time to talk to the British Government. A friend of mine, Michael Heseltine, a Minister in Edward Heath's Government, arranged for me to meet a high official in the Home Office.

I flew to London on Thursday, January 27, 1972 to discuss my proposals in detail. There was immediate interest, even enthusiasm. Could I clarify some points? Would the IRA agree to a cease-fire on the *promise* of internment ending? Would this allow talks to take place? How interested was Paisley? The Home Office official made copious notes. He left the room a number of times on some pretext or another. The significance of this only dawned on me some days later when I discovered that Brian Faulkner, Northern Ireland's Prime Minister, had flown over from Belfast that same morning and was, in fact, in the very next room being kept informed on the discussions.

Then a question. Could I stay overnight while my proposals were considered by the British Government?

I was excited and encouraged by this development. A cease-fire might even be arranged by the weekend.

I stayed that night. Called back the following morning. No, it was just was not possible. So many imponderables. How sure could they be that the truce would be maintained? What if the talks broke down?

I was infuriated and depressed by the response, the apparent intransigence, and flew home on 28 January, dejected, feeling in my heart that a real opportunity to solve the problem had been lost. Forty eight hours later it was Bloody Sunday, January 30, 1972, and 13 people on a civil rights march in Derry were shot dead by British paratroopers.

The repercussions of Bloody Sunday were dramatic. Twenty-five thousand people marched on the British Embassy in Dublin and burned it down. I remember watching the battalions of marchers converging on Merrion Square and marvelling at the power of nationalism to arouse the feelings of ordinary Irish people — feelings I had found it impossible to arouse on burning social issues like the plight of Dublin's homeless a few years previously.

The impact of Bloody Sunday was felt throughout the world, particularly in the United States, where anti-British feeling ran high among Irish-Americans and proposals for Senate Committee Hearings on Northern Ireland won overwhelming support.

Spearheading these moves were Senators Ted Kennedy and Abe Ribicoff, and because of my involvement in the abortive peace plan, I was invited to Washington on February 26, 1972 to observe these hearings. The findings were inconclusive.

However, two particular incidents still stick in my mind.

I remember when Ted Kennedy moved on stage at the hearings. TV cameras were rolled in, the lights came on, and crowds packed the galleries. After a fiery speech demanding justice for the people of Ireland, Kennedy was gone and so were the cameras, the lights, and the crowds — an indication of the Kennedy charisma.

Senator Abe Ribicoff stood up to follow Kennedy's performance but the departure of the Senator from Massachussetts had deprived the hearings of their glamour and excitement. However, Ribicoff soldiered on, reading a prepared speech which concentrated, in large part, on the efforts an Irish Parliamentarian, Dr John O'Connell, had made with the peace plan which might have averted Bloody Sunday. I must confess that I felt very flattered and immediately his speech was ended I went over to introduce myself.

"I'm the Dr O'Connell you referred to in your speech," I said, brimming with expectation.

"Oh, hi," he said and then he brushed past me and was gone. A chastening lesson for the swollen-headed O'Connell, and a realisation that Ribicoff's speech was merely a theatrical exercise.

Six weeks later, in March 1972, Republican leaders, Sean Mac Stiofain, David O'Connell and Joe Cahill contacted me and asked if I could bring a document to the attention of the British government. It was in connection with a seventy-two hour truce they proposed to call. The document was one page long. Scraps of it still stick in my mind. The British army were to withdraw to barracks and not to engage in any hostile acts or provocation.

I read it, folded it, stuffed it back in my pocket and went in search of the telephone number of Harold Wilson, then leader of the British Labour Party. Because of my party's fraternal links with the British Labour Party I telephoned. Could I talk to Harold Wilson? John O'Connell, Labour MP in Dublin. Yes, hold on. I held on. The familiar voice, laconic, non-committal.

"I have a document from the IRA that I've been asked to bring to the attention of the British Government."

"Can you come over immediately with it?"

"Well, I could come tomorrow morning."

"Fine, I'll see you at my home at eleven. No 5, Lord North Street, London."

I took an early plane the following morning, March 9, 1972 and a taxi from the airport. The taxi crashed halfway to his house. The driver was injured, the place thick with policemen, and there was I with this document (very likely personally incriminating, I thought later, as a copy of this document found in the possession of an IRA suspect led to his conviction) burning a hole in my pocket.

Eventually, I was free to take another taxi. Wilson opened the door himself.

"You must be Doctor O'Connell."

I had a sudden, irreverent urge to say "And you must be Harold Wilson." I suppressed it.

"I'm lucky to have got here at all. My taxi crashed."

"Oh! You must be very shocked. Have a glass of brandy."

"I don't drink."

"Oh. Well, then, I'll have a glass of brandy."

Brandy poured.

"May I see the document."

The document simply stated that the IRA proposed to call a 72-hour truce under certain conditions

He read it in silence. Re-read it. Read it again.

"What do you think of this?"

"I'm not sure. But it's a start."

"I'm going to show this to Mr Heath, the Prime Minister, in Privy Council." (Apparently anything said in Privy Council is never revealed to the public).

He took me in his car to Leicester Square, where we both alighted. He led me by the elbow to a restaurant. I was suddenly acutely conscious of the double-takes of people around me. Could that be Harold Wilson? Live? In the flesh?

"Go in here," he said, nodding at the restaurant, "and tell the chef I sent you, and you'll get a decent steak. Come to the House of Commons at two thirty and I'll see you in my rooms there."

His rooms, when I found them later, were, I recall, large, dark and gloomy. Wood panelling and heavy old fashioned furniture, a great green-topped desk and armchairs, combined to give a heavy, depressing effect. MPs came and went.

"I showed the document to the Prime Minister, Mr Heath," he said. A small pause. "Can you arrange for me to meet the Republicans?"

"Yes," I said impulsively, not having a clue as to whether or not I might be able to deliver on the promise.

"I have a long-standing engagement to do an interview with Irish television, and I can go over next Monday on the pretext of doing that interview, and meet them. Could you arrange for the meeting to be very private. What about your house?"

"Yes of course," I replied.

He then went on to suggest changes in the wording of the document, the significance of which passed over my head. To this day, I can remember neither those details nor the reasons for them. I simply noted them on the document with a biro.

Merlyn Rees, Wilson's Shadow Minister on Northern Ireland, arrived, and was told about what was going on. Rees said little, and I formed the impression of a weak man, rather a sycophant in Wilson's presence. An ageing boy, in political terms. Labour M.P. Kevin McNamara also came and went, and appeared to be very curious about my presence. It appears he was Labour's junior spokesman on Northern Ireland but Wilson and particularly Rees, were not anxious to involve him in the discussions.

I returned home, and as had been arranged with David O'Connell, I went to see him at a house in Blackrock. The newspapers often called him "Daithi" but he always announced himself to me as David. It was now well after midnight. I found O'Connell oddly impressive. More reasonable than his public statements would lead one to believe, more thoughtful, more likely to compromise if the gains made were sufficient.

I handed him the document, now rather dog-eared. He read it silently, noting my biro-ed changes.

"Obviously you've been successful in bringing this to the British Government."

"I brought it to Harold Wilson and he told me he had shown it to Prime Minister Mr Heath in Privy Council, and he suggested the changes."

"It shouldn't be impossible to include these changes in the conditions for our 72-hour truce." Relaxed he was, satisfied.

I told him about Wilson's desire to meet them the following Monday with a view to extending the truce. He listened impassively.

"I'll have to bring your request to the leaders of the Republican Movement. I will let you know, Dr O'Connell."

"But this man is coming here on Monday for the express purpose of seeing you. I have more or less given him an undertaking that you'll meet him."

"The leadership of the Republican Movement will have to decide that. I will contact you."

He gave me a special number to phone on Saturday at a special time. I was desperately agitated, fearful that I had committed Wilson to what might turn out to be a fruitless journey. What would I do if they decided against meeting him? I went home. The following afternoon I telephoned David O'Connell at the pre-arranged time.

"I'm sorry. No decision has been reached yet. I cannot tell you anything now. Telephone this number again on Monday".

I occupied myself by arranging the RTE interview by telephone. The person there obviously thought I was some representative of Wilson's, and made no connection with John O'Connell, TD. Then it was Monday, March 13, and Wilson was on his way, but I still had no decision from the "leadership of the Republican Movement". The various political parties, Fianna Fáil, Fine Gael and Labour or rather representatives of each, were to meet him. I requested that I be included in the Labour Party group to meet Wilson. Request denied.

The Labour Party was to meet him in Leinster House, and with a few minutes to go before Wilson's arrival, Brendan Corish was standing in the front hall, anxiously looking out the window on to Merrion Square. I stood talking to him. It was obvious he wanted me to go away, and eventually he said so.

"I'd better go John. I've got to see him now," he said curtly as Wilson's car drove up. I was still in the front hall of Leinster House as Wilson arrived, flanked by Tony Field (brother of Marcia Williams, later Lady Falkender) and his political adviser, Joe Haines. Wilson glanced at me, and I gave him a blank look of non-recognition.

His eyes moved on, never changing expression. Tony Field got near enough to me to mutter — "Is the meeting OK for tonight?"

"Yes," I said with more hope than confidence.

"Harold wants to see you for dinner in his room at the Shelbourne."

"OK."

I was like a hen on a hot griddle from then until five o'clock, the time set for me to phone David O'Connell to see if a decision had been reached by "the leadership of the Republican Movement". I had the phrase learned off by heart. At five, I phoned.

"John O'Connell here."

"Yes, We've agreed to meet Mr Wilson in your house. Also, we want to be in your house beforehand. We will arrive by eight thirty. We don't want to meet the Special Branch who'll be arriving with him. Oh, and another thing—"

My heart sank — an impossible condition, no doubt.

"Would it be possible to have a television set there, so we can watch his interview?"

Vast relief.

"Sure, yes, I'll arrange that."

My family was pressed into service to prepare some food for the meeting.

I went along to the Shelbourne Hotel to meet Wilson, relieved that whatever might be the final outcome, I had at least fulfilled my part of the mission without goofing. I prayed that in the time before the meeting there would be no mistakes, no hitches.

"John, that's all arranged, is it?" was Wilson's greeting, as I arrived at his room in the hotel. I nodded in what I hoped was a calmly convinced manner. With Joe Haines and Merlyn Rees, we had dinner, and I told Wilson about the Sinn Féin request for a TV screen to watch his interview.

"Oh," he said thoughtfully, like a man doing mental arithmetic. "Oh, I must be very careful that I don't say anything on television that might antagonise them. John, can you be outside the television station after the interview?"

I nodded.

"What kind of car have you?"

I described it.

"Well, the British Embassy car will be parked outside RTE You pull up directly behind it and park. As I leave the building, I'll pretend I am going to the Embassy car, but at the last second, I'll switch to your car instead. Then we'll follow the Embassy car for a little way, and after that, we can branch off, and you'll take me directly to your house."

After that, the dinner in his room was purely social, and very pleasant. Wilson was charming. Rees, then the British Labour Party spokesman for Northern Ireland, justified my first impression of him as a man with a role but without a contribution by offering little or nothing. It was clear that for the moment at least, although Rees might, in name, be their man on the North, in fact, that job was Wilson's. Then the group split up. Wilson headed for Donnybrook and the interview with Liam Hourican while I drove home, to find the Sinn Féin delegation had just arrived. I offered them food and drinks, and got refusals. They watched the TV in our dining room. Then I drove to RTE, where, as arranged, I parked behind the Embassy car. A member of the Special Branch promptly arrived beside my window.

"Look, I'm bringing Mr Wilson to my house for a drink after his interview," I explained, "so I wonder if you could sort of disperse in the garden of my home because I think he'd like a little privacy."

The Special Branch man looked thoughtful.

"Dr O'Connell, how long will he be in your house? A few hours?"

"Yes."

"How sure are you?"

"Very sure. Positive."

"Well, if you ARE sure, then I think we could move away and leave him to it, provided we have had an absolute assurance that he won't leave before midnight."

I gave the assurance, and not long afterwards, Wilson came rapidly through the tall glass doors with RTE Director-General Tom Hardiman, and a retinue of other RTE officials to see him off. As arranged, he changed direction and climbed into my car. I drove quickly, and, arriving at the house, drove up the driveway. For a second, suspicion crossed Wilson's face as he registered the dark garden and the tall house. My house was situated on its own grounds away from the main road.

"Where's this?"

"My house."

"Forbidding place, your house."

Joe Haines, his political aide, was later to say that Wilson's suspicions arose from his knowledge that 90 years previously the Chief Secretary for Ireland, Frederick Cavendish, was assassinated at the Phoenix Park not far from my house, and they were uncertain of what was in store for them. We entered the room where the IRA leaders were already sitting at one end of a long table.

"I don't know that we need to go through the formality of introductions," Wilson said, seating himself at the head of the table, and placing me to his right. Merlyn Rees, Joe Haines, and Tony Field sat on his left. At the other end of the table sat David O'Connell, Joe Cahill, and John Kelly.

As the talks started, Wilson discreetly passed to me a sheet of paper on which were drawn three circles and written underneath "Who is who?" I put names under the circles. Within minutes, he had made some comment to Joe Cahill, the import of which passed me by, but which evidently showed inside knowledge of what had happened to Cahill on a recent trip to the United States. Cahill was startled.

"You're not far off the mark," he said, with a grudging smile.

Wilson referred to the IRA truce which had been going on for seventy-two hours, as promised in the original document which I had taken back and forth across the Irish Sea. The IRA had implemented the truce.

133

"I have to admit, you know something about discipline," he remarked. "You can certainly turn a war on and off when you want."

The talk ranged over every aspect of the Northern problem, and I was very impressed by how much Wilson knew. Either he took a deep and genuine interest in the situation, or someone had briefed him perfectly. The discussion was businesslike, almost cordial, and there was a guarded agreement suggested by me that there should be further meetings, in private. Near midnight, the Sinn Féin men asked if Wilson would leave first. I drove him back to the Shelbourne, the Special branch men flashing the headlights of their cars as we took off, to let me know where they were. Wilson asked if I would have breakfast with him next morning at nine o'clock, and I returned to my house, where the "leadership of the Republican Movement" had unbent sufficiently to have a cup of tea. Joe Cahill had a little pocket radio with him, and at one o'clock he tuned it to the BBC news, taking a little card from his pocket as he did so.

The first item on the news dealt with the bombings in the North which had resumed at midnight as soon as the 72-hour truce had ended, one hour before. Cahill silently marked little ticks on his card as each bombing incident was named.

They talked of the meeting, at which their central, recurring theme had been "Stormont must go." (Ironically enough Heath announced the abolition of Stormont eleven days later on March 24, 1972 along with the appointment of William Whitelaw as Secretary of State for Northern Ireland. The gradual release of internees followed.) They seemed both enthusiastic about the way the meeting had gone and intrigued by Wilson's knowledge.

"He's certainly well-informed," one of them remarked. Then they were gone, and the house was silent.

Next morning, I went to the Shelbourne, and found Wilson in an optimistic frame of mind.

"Isn't David O'Connell very politically oriented?" he commented. "I was very impressed by him."

He said he was happy with the visit, and that he and I should keep in regular contact, giving me a special number so that I

134

might get straight through to him if necessary. A photograph was taken of Harold Wilson and myself, then he gave me his firm handshake, and that was the end of it. I assumed that this was the end of the episode, and was taken aback when, eight days later, on March 21, Wilson telephoned to tell me that there was going to be a special debate on the Northern situation in the House of Commons that day and he was going to announce in the House what had happened in Dublin. I was very upset. I knew I would be in trouble, and I was right. The three o'clock BBC news carried the report of what he had said, and by two minutes past three, all hell was breaking loose. The TV people, the Press, the radio reporters were all on to me wanting comment. I said I had little to say, but I did not deny that the meeting had taken place. Nor did I deny orchestrating it. Interviewed, I refused to name the people who had taken part.

My party, meanwhile, was in a collective froth of fury. Someone told me that Brendan Corish wanted me in his office "immediately if not sooner." When I got there he was in a towering temper.

"What you have done," he stormed, "has been a betrayal of party policy, and the whip will be removed from you tomorrow morning, first thing."

I was deeply, deeply upset.

"Brendan, I didn't realise that."

I was cut short. Later (to my shame, I now feel with hindsight), I went back three times to beg that this should not be done to me. What did not occur to me at the time was that he had no right to pre-empt what the Party would decide to do with me. Removing the whip is a party decision, not done on a Leader's whim. Luckily enough, things began to happen which changed the atmosphere somewhat. It was evident very quickly that whatever the Labour Party felt about their backbencher meeting the Provos with Wilson, the general public was happy that someone was trying to do something to try to halt the carnage in the North. A delegation from the Irish Transport and General Workers Union executive called to the Dáil to let it be known to Corish that if any motion was passed expelling me, they would disaffiliate from the Party. This I didn't know until later.

At the Party meetings things were stormy. I refused to name the people at the meeting in my house, and above all the other condemning voices, the clear, articulate fury of Conor Cruise O'Brien rose and dominated.

"This attitude of O'Connell's is ridiculous; what he's done is unforgivable."

"I'm sorry," I said. "I regard myself as honour bound to say no more than that the leadership of the Republican movement was there."

"He mustn't be allowed to take refuge in this so-called undertaking," O'Brien said. (He never at this meeting addressed me directly.) "He's got to be FORCED to explain himself."

I began to feel sick inside. Ten other voices made themselves heard. Michael Pat Murphy, Labour's TD from West Cork, lowered the decibel level by his combination of a low, soft voice and his determination to get his way.

"I don't know that what John O'Connell did was wrong at all," he said in the quiet but steely Cork accent. "I know I felt proud, when I heard down in my area that it wasn't the Taoiseach or the Fianna Fáil Party or Fine Gael that had arranged that meeting, but one of our own. My people weren't unhappy about it at all. I really don't know that John O'Connell did anything wrong."

It was the first sign that the Party was not in complete unanimity on the question of my expulsion. Then Senator Jack Fitzgerald, a solid Party member and a loyal friend of Brendan Corish spoke.

"I want to make it perfectly clear that if any action is taken to expel John O'Connell, I will resign from the Party."

This, coming from him, heartened me considerably. I suddenly realised that the motion for my expulsion might not be moved, or that if it was moved, it might be beaten. In the end, the motion was never moved, mainly because of the Transport Union intervention and the input from Michael Pat Murphy and Senator Fitzgerald. Conor Cruise O'Brien stamped out. I came out of the meeting, weak from the sustained tension, to find a battery of pressmen gathered for information.

"Would you do the same again, should the occasion arise?" they asked.

"If I thought any fruitful discussions would take place, I'd do it again like a shot," I replied.

Controversy raged for some months, during which time I kept up covert contact with Wilson. I was becoming a little more knowledgeable about the North, spending a great deal of time there, talking to anybody, politician or lay person, who wanted to talk with me, going into Protestant and Catholic ghettoes, meeting Taylor, Paisley — and Cardinal Conway.

My meeting with the Cardinal was somewhat stormy, since I had made a speech not long before, attacking segregated education. When I knelt to kiss the Cardinal's ring, he brushed me aside so impatiently that I slipped on the polished floor and almost fell full-length. He then attacked me about my speech, in which I had suggested that the established churches bore heavy responsibility for the present troubles. He was in a towering rage, unprepared for any kind of conversation.

"Your Eminence," I said, rising from the small armchair he had positioned me in, "You're behaving like a fifteen year old schoolboy, and I see little point in further discussion."

That was my only direct contact with the late Cardinal, although I must add that later, when a proposal to solve the Northern problem was outlined to him, and it was stated that it had come from me, he was warm and supportive about it.

Towards the end of March 1972, Mr. Wilson arranged that I should see Whitelaw, then Northern Secretary, to discuss the northern situation. The IRA wanted me to see him, not to bring up specific proposals but to talk to him about certain aspects of the troubles. Before I went up to Belfast I saw Joe Cahill.

"Where do you think I should stay while in Belfast?" I asked, knowing it would require forty eight hours. He thought for a moment, then told me not to stay in one hotel, nor in a second nor in a third. He then named a fourth.

"Stay there," he said. "Make sure you stay there."

That night, the other three were bombed.

Some time afterwards, Wilson asked if the Republican leaders would meet him again, and said that he would send over a private plane to take them, and me, to his home in Great Missinden, outside Luton. This time, the major fear in my mind was of flying. The thought of a little private plane made me positively sick with fear. "It's important that you do this" I said to myself. "Shape up." This time the Republican leadership would not let David O'Connell go, to his disappointment and my dismay. I liked his attitude, his way of thinking and his personal charm. Instead, the little private plane took off from Weston Airdrome with three hardliners on July 18, 1972. My confidence about flying was further diminished when there was a conversation between the pilot and a local man about getting cattle off the field before we could move.

I was terrified all the way across, to such an extent that I indulged in precious little speculation as to what would happen at the meeting. I was just concerned with landing at Luton Airport in one piece.

When we arrived at Wilson's house, the Republican leaders were guided to a converted bar, which Wilson had made into a conference room, while he took time out to walk around the grounds, showing me with some pride all the alterations he had made to the house and gardens. The tension of the flight combined with excessive tiredness from the preceding days' work made me sleepy. I fought to maintain a clear head but during the discussions, the desire to sleep became overpowering. I must have spent nearly half that meeting, head pillowed on arms, fast asleep. That's the effect flying has on me. Afterwards, Wilson was less than ebullient.

"Hardliners," he said tersely. "Hardliners, every one of them. What a pity David O'Connell wasn't here."

We set off home, the journey seeming shorter than the outward leg. At Dublin Airport, where we landed for customs purposes, the customs man looked in the plane and registered the faces of the three men with me.

"We've brought nothing with us," I said. He looked searchingly at me.

"That's all right, Dr. O'Connell."

We were free to fly down to Weston, and this time, for some crazy reason, I ended up guiding the English pilot, picking out areas on the ground familiar to me in Ballyfermot and Palmerstown, and indicating his route to him.

After the meeting in Wilson's home at Great Missinden, from which nothing seemed to come, there was continued contact with him. More initiatives. Some of them ideas of mine. Sean McBride, I thought. Respected by the IRA, I knew. If he asked them to stop the bombing, maybe they would. But would he? I phoned Wilson. Great idea, he said. Go to it. I contacted McBride. He came to my office to talk about it, and I told him of my conviction that progress could be made in new talks on the situation only if the bombing could be halted.

"Look, Sean, the IRA hold you in very high regard. I know they're very much influenced by what you do and say. This senseless murder has got to stop, and you're the only person in this country I can think of who could persuade them to stop. If you do this for me, I guarantee that Wilson will ensure that meaningful talks will take place on reaching a solution to the whole problem."

We talked for an hour. At the end of it, Sean McBride said yes, he would go to see one of the hardliners he knew, and see what he could do to persuade him. Later, he phoned me to say he had spoken to the person concerned and he believed he had got from him an undertaking that the bombing would stop. Wilson had asked me to phone him at the Adelphi Hotel, Liverpool, where he was staying. I phoned Wilson, great relief. Then I went to see Republican leader, Joe Cahill, in Templeogue for corroboration of McBride's understanding that the IRA bombing campaign was about to stop. Cahill had just returned to Dublin after a two day trip to Belfast and was struggling with a TV connection, trying to make it work when I called on him. I took the connection from him, since it was evident that he was not going to concentrate on anything until the TV was working, and I rigged it up for him. He switched on the UTV news. I was bubbling with what I wanted to say and ask and it took a moment for the announcer's words to sink in.

It was Bloody Friday in Belfast and they were counting the dead and putting the pieces in plastic bags after twenty car bomb explosions. I turned sick and giddy.

"That's terrible, terrible," I muttered.

"That's the way it's got to be," Cahill said blandly.

"How could you?" I cried, desperately. "How could you?"

But even as I said it, the memory came back to me of him with his little card in my house neatly ticking off the exploded bombs after the March 1972 truce had ended.

Some time later, I went into the Republicans' bad books because, during the time of the Sean MacStiofain hunger strike, I was asked in public what I would do in the circumstances, and I said that as a doctor, I would feel obliged to put up an intravenous drip. MacStiofain told the IRA to have nothing to do with me, which was particularly ironic, in view of the fact that about this time a myth began to build up of John O'Connell, Provo sympathiser, which could not have been further from the truth.

Nevertheless, I was determined not to give up, and when David O'Connell approached me about conditions for Republican prisoners in Portlaoise Prison, I broached the subject of some initiatives which might result in a permanent cease-fire. He was receptive to the idea. I then discussed my idea of a Three-Man Commission being set up by the British government with the power to hold discussions in private with all interested groups in Northern Ireland, elected and non-elected, and to make recommendations which would be binding on all parties including the British government.

The Commission, as I envisaged it, would hold its deliberations in private, away from the glare of the media. I felt this was vital as it would enable political leaders and others to be much more forthcoming since they would not be forced to adopt a hardline public stance. My experience of talking with many of these leaders was that their private views were so very often different from their public utterances. To persuade the hardliners on both sides to accept such a Commission, I felt it would be necessary to include in it public figures who would have the trust of the respective camps. I reasoned that the man the IRA would trust on such a Commission was Sean McBride, and got him to agree to the hypothetical arrangement before approaching Desmond Boal, a senior lawyer in Northern

Ireland and one time policy adviser to Ian Paisley. I considered him the figure most likely to be acceptable to hardline Unionists. He too agreed, saying it was the best idea he had come upon for a long time. And a person of the stature of a British ex-Minister might be accepted to represent the British Government's position on this Commission.

By this time Harold Wilson was Prime Minister, having been elected in February 1974, and I felt certain he would be receptive to my proposal because of the great concern he had shown while in opposition. At this time also, David O'Connell confided in me about the Feakle Peace Talks with the Protestant Churchmen of the North — talks which were expected to bring in their wake a temporary cease-fire. I felt that this cease-fire could be extended indefinitely if Wilson would give his imprimatur to the Three-Man Commission. It seemed to me to be imperative that the cease-fire not be jeopardised. I emphasised this to James Allen, Britain's senior civil servant in the North, and was rather surprised at his indifferent attitude.

The leadership of the Republican movement ordered a unilateral suspension of offensive military action in Britain and Northern Ireland on 22 December, 1974. Surprise turned into alarm when David O'Connell contacted me to say that due to bungling on the part of Frank Cooper, the Permanent Under-Secretary of Sate, the truce was in grave danger of breaking down, and that it was very important that the British Government be informed of the reasons for the imminent resumption of hostilities. The news flash on Thursday, 16 January 1975 on Ulster Television announcing that the truce was to end at midnight, goaded me into immediate action.

I telephoned Tony Field (the brother of Marcia Williams and one-time office manager for Harold Wilson) at 6 p.m. and asked him if he could get the message directly through to Prime Minister Harold Wilson at Number 10 Downing Street. This he agreed to do. He promised to phone me back at 9.00 p.m. However, within an hour of my speaking to Tony Field, James Allen, Britain's chief civil servant in the North, phoned my home. I was taken aback when he informed me that he was aware of and annoyed at my making direct contact with the

Prime Minister. As I discovered later, the civil servants in Downing Street had intercepted Tony Field's private talk with Wilson and had subsequently relayed its contents directly to Allen.

Tony Field, as promised, phoned me at 9.00 p.m. to say that Prime Minister Wilson had received the message and was arranging for the appointment of a personal contact man between him and me, a man by the name of Albert (who I discovered later was Albert Murray) who was to phone me the following day. But in fact I had a phone call one hour later from this man Albert who told me that he was available to convey all messages directly to the Prime Minister and that I could phone him at any time of the day or night.

He also gave me his personal phone number at Ten Downing Street and his home number in Gravesend. He said he was available to come to Dublin if necessary to discuss with the Republican leaders how the truce could be maintained. I immediately advised the IRA of this new contact and that night I was brought before the Army Council. They asked me if I could bring a personal letter from the Army Council directly across to Prime Minister Wilson because they said they had no trust in either Merlyn Rees, now Secretary of State for Northern Ireland, or in his representatives in the North, Sir Frank Cooper and James Allen. I agreed to do so, and phoned Albert Murray at eleven o'clock that same night about the IRA request. He said that Prime Minister Wilson would be prepared to accept the letter only if the IRA agreed to extend the truce which was due to expire that night. I persuaded the IRA to extend the truce and the following morning I flew to London. In London, the episode took on the flavour of a spy thriller. I was instructed to stand outside the Old Vic Theatre at a given time and was told that a British Government car would pick me up. A car duly arrived with Joe Haines, Wilson's political adviser (whom I had met when Wilson came to Dublin in March, 1972) and Wilson's "go-between," Albert Murray.

I was taken to a private office where it was explained to me by Joe Haines and Albert Murray that confidential messages from me to Wilson had been withheld from the Prime Minister by certain civil servants in Number 10 Downing Street and that Wilson had only suddenly come upon them a few days previously. I mentioned the fact that my message to Tony Field, relayed directly by him to Number Ten, had been intercepted by the civil servants and leaked to their man in the North, James Allen. Both Haines and Albert Murray agreed that the civil servants were leaking this information and that they found it difficult to stop it.

I was asked to elaborate on my proposal for the Three-Man Commission for Northern Ireland and my progress to date on it, as details I had previously submitted had mysteriously disappeared in Number Ten. I was then asked to remain at the Strand Palace hotel while the IRA confidential letter was brought to Wilson in Chequers. The IRA letter is reproduced in the appendix at the end of this book. It clearly indicated that unless meaningful initiatives were taken by Wilson himself, the truce would have to end but that bombing on the mainland (Britain) would not be resumed. A few hours later, Albert Murray returned from Chequers to the Strand Palace Hotel and asked me to clarify some points in the IRA letter to the Prime Minister.

This I was unable to do other than to speculate on what the IRA might have in mind. What became apparent to me at that time was that the paragraph in the letter stating that there would be no bombing in Britain was a great source of relief to the Prime Minister and his aides. To me, it seemed, they were indifferent to the fact that bombing might be resumed in Northern Ireland so long as Britain was spared. I was given to understand that the question of the Three-Man Commission in Northern Ireland was still under consideration.

And then, it all quietly faded away. Nothing happened. I had taken the idea as far as I could without becoming a crank about it, and I had to leave it alone. I did meet Wilson, quite by accident, in a restaurant in London, in August 1978. There had been no contact between us for a long time and we talked briefly. I reminded him of his once-expressed ambition to go down in history as the Prime Minister who solved the Northern problem.

"What a pity," I said, "that you didn't take the necessary steps to achieve that ambition."

"I have no interest there anymore," he said coldly, and that was the end of it.

There are a few aspects of the British Government's policy on Northern Ireland that have never failed to puzzle me. The British Government, despite public declarations to the contrary, were prepared to talk to and even negotiate with the IRA, as they did on a number of occasions. Yet there always seemed to be some power operating behind the scenes, of which British politicians were vaguely aware but unable to control.

That power could be the Army, the civil service, big business interests or a combination of the three, but my impression was always that many British politicians seriously wanted to extricate themselves from Northern Ireland, but the "colonial" influence of the British Establishment was too strong.

I was never a theoretician on Northern Ireland. I never claimed to have a unique insight into the Northern problem. My involvement was based on one simple principle — get people talking instead of shooting and bombing, save lives instead of adding to the statistics of tragedy. It was that principle which brought me to Bobby Sands' deathbed.

# Chapter 7

# Bobby Sands

David O'Connell of Sinn Fein. He kept in touch with me regularly from the first time he contacted me in 1971 about the arranging of the meeting with Harold Wilson. He was in contact with me a good deal in '74 about a truce in the North that almost broke down a couple of times. When that happened, he would come up to me in a hurry to see who I could influence.

He would come to my house disguised, and he often came through the downstairs window. A rapport grew between us. I believed that he sincerely wanted a political role for the IRA and we talked about that. There were elections coming in Northern Ireland and I wondered aloud during one of his visits, about the possibility of the British Government actually supporting the establishment of Sinn Fein advice centres or facilitating their set-up. They were badly needed, because most Sinn Féin candidates had been interned and they would be at a disadvantage vis-a-vis the other candidates in elections. By having advice centres I was hoping their organisation would become politicized, thereby steering them away from their military activities. Money may not have been won from the British Government, but I suspect that some money did come through the Roantree Trust for one of these centres. What emerged, as I remember, was that these so-called advice centres became in effect, patrol-centres controlled by the IRA.

In 1981, more than a decade after the Northern troubles began, Republican prisoners went on a sustained hunger strike in the Maze which focused the eyes of the world on the prison and left ten of them dead.

Hunger strikes were no new thing in Ireland, particularly for Republicans. In 1917, prisoners in Mountjoy refused to eat as part of a protest related to prison clothes and prison work. Thomas Ashe, their 32-year old leader, died as a result of force-feeding. Three years later, the Lord Mayor of Cork, Terence Mc Swiney, who was an officer commanding a local brigade of the IRA in Cork, was captured by British troops at an IRA meeting and sentenced to two years in prison. He went on hunger strike as a way of rejecting the jurisdiction of the British in Ireland. The hunger strike fit in with his personal patriotic philosophy, which held that Ireland needed to be inspired by great sacrifices. The length of this hunger strike became legendary. McSwiney died on the seventy-fourth day of it.

The Northern hunger strikers in the early Eighties had adopted one of McSwiney's strongest beliefs: that the Republican struggle is not like traditional war. In this conflict, McSwiney said, "it is not those who can inflict the most, but those that can suffer the most who will conquer."

From 1969 onwards, a hunger strike was always a possible weapon on the Republican side in the North. In the Maze prison, at the beginning of the Eighties, there were over a thousand prisoners, the majority of them Republicans. They had been imprisoned as a result of what had been called the "criminalization strategy" of the British Government, which had done away with juries and softened the rules of evidence to make conviction easier. The Republican movement felt that since these men had been convicted by special courts and by procedures which, *ipso facto*, recognised their crimes as political, then, in prison, they should have similar special category status. The authorities refused. These men were treated as common criminals and forced to carry out menial tasks — something they strongly objected to.

From within the prison a message was coming for the Army Council: "Let us go on hunger strike. It has worked before." At the time the Pope visited Ireland, the pressure was at an all-time high, and ten volunteers had been selected from among the prisoners. But the Army Council still held off, believing that the

146

special category status problem could be resolved in other ways. No progress was made, and a now forgotten episode involving a Welshman tipped the balance towards starvation and death for the prisoners.

What happened was that the Conservative Party in Britain had refused to honour a pledge made in an election manifesto that a Welsh-language station would be part of the new fourth television channel. Gwynfor Evans, President of Plaid Cymru, the Welsh Nationalist Party, threatened to go on hunger strike in protest. He was sixty seven years of age. Two weeks before the strike was due to start, Home Secretary Willie Whitelaw caved in and agreed that Wales would get the TV service Evans wanted. If Evans could do it by threat, then, went the argument from the Republican prisoners, we can do it in reality. One prisoner had already been on a more personally motivated hunger strike which had lasted for more than sixty days, so the prisoners knew precisely what was involved in physical and psychological terms — as did the prison authorities.

On the tenth of October, 1980, the permission came from the Army Council, and it was announced that a hunger strike would be launched just over a fortnight later. At the time of the announcement, the implications of the decision were unclear to the general public. It was about an improvement in prison conditions, but it was about a lot more than that, as journalist David Beresford was to point out in his book, *Ten Men Dead*.

> Hunger-striking, when taken to the death, has a sublime quality about it; in conjunction with terrorism it offers a consummation of murder and selfsacrifice which in a sense can legitimize the violence which precedes and follows it. If after killing — or sharing in a conspiracy to kill — for a cause one shows oneself willing to die for the same cause, a value is adduced which is higher than that of life itself. But the obverse is also true; failure to die can discredit the cause. To scream for mercy at the foot of the gallows — or nod at the saline drip as kidneys and eyes collapse and the doctor warns of irreversible damage — is to affirm that there is no higher value than life and none more worthy of condemnation than those who take it.

The prisoners wanted the strike. If they did not have it, said one of them, a round faced young man named Bobby Sands,

147

"The H-Blocks could become the knacker's yard of the Republican Movement." That first hunger strike went on, but for various reasons, the strikers were out-manoeuvred and the effort collapsed. But at the beginning of 1981 the plans were in position for a much more sustained strike which nobody could outmanoeuvre.

By March 1981, men were already starving and sending each other little secret messages of support. The newspapers, nationally and internationally, were becoming interested, and the general public was growing familiar, as a result of posters wrapped around lampposts with the blurred cheery chubby face of prisoner Bobby Sands, now on hunger strike, who had, while in prison, been elected a member of the British parliament.

I was then a Member of the European Parliament. But although I had to spend much of my time in Europe, I had not lost touch with David O'Connell, and from the beginning of the hunger strike, he talked, at first vaguely, and then more urgently, about what a good idea it would be for me to come up and see the prisoners and visit the Maze. About four or five weeks later, listening to the very early morning news on the BBC, I heard that I had been invited, together with Neil Blaney and Sile de Valera, to visit Bobby Sands. None of us knew how close he was to death, but it was clear that it might be days, rather than weeks away. The invitation had come from the Prisoners' Support Group.

I knew Neil Blaney well as an ardent Republican. In addition, I had known him as a very competent Minister for Local Government. Sile de Valera at the time was a member of the European Parliament — as indeed was Neil Blaney — and, because I never confined my friendships to Labour Party people, but also got on well with other political party members, I had talked with her often, and found her to be a very warm-hearted, committed and intelligent person. I was always slightly awed by the de Valera name, but you could not be awed by Sile; she has too much self-deprecatory humour for that. You could talk about anything with her, and if you needed something done which she could help you with, she facilitated you and made no fuss about it.

I assume it was David O'Connell who had suggested my name as a person to be invited to the Maze. I had open lines of communication to the IRA, and they knew that I could fight for a man's rights without necessarily agreeing with his beliefs. We had a conversation about three weeks before the call and as I got dressed that morning, wondering what to do, I linked the invitation to that conversation. I phoned Sile and we made arrangements. In this instance, I felt I was going up there, not for political purposes, but very specifically in my role as a doctor. And so my first aim had to be to try and persuade Sands (and other prisoners if we met them) to give up the hunger strike.

Later that day, we received a phone call saying we should go to the Fairways Hotel beyond Dundalk and just south of the border early the following morning, and that we would be met there. There was no chance that this visit would be kept secret from start to finish, but a secret it was at that time. I had been working with Mr Haughey in trying to resolve the problem of the hunger strike, but I did not let him know in advance that I was going to the Maze, for fear of creating an irrelevant controversy.

I must have gone to the Fairways about 6.30 and had breakfast there. Sile de Valera and Neil Blaney then arrived, and shortly afterwards, two members of Sinn Fein. If I remember rightly, one of the two was Danny Morrissey, the other Owen Carron, who was Bobby Sands's election agent when Sands had become an MP. They told us there was a car outside the door, and that we would be driven to the border by two Sinn Fein people. We were then to be picked up by an RUC team. We were just driven over the border. The car stopped. Another car reversed towards us — the RUC vehicle — we got into it and set off in silence along a route lined with men, either RUC or British Army, very visibly armed. In a space of 100 yards there would be 50 of them. There was little else on the road, because it was too early for daily business to have started.

After a journey of about thirty miles, we came to the Maze Prison and of course we were searched. Frisked. A new experience for me, this efficient if cursory personal invasion.

Remember, we were all three of us members of the European Parliament. That had a certain status because the British could not possibly have refused us access to the prison. Yet they frisked us as if we were likely to be carrying weapons. We stood, startled into immobility. Not one of us objected. Each one of us coloured and avoided eye contact with the others.

Then we were put into a van, and locked into it as we were brought through the grounds. I hated that. Not because of the affront to our collective dignity. I tend to look at things first in terms of practicalities, and my initial reaction was simply that locking people inside a van with no escape route in the event of an accident was hazardous. Looking at the tiny back window, I was made edgy by the knowledge that none of us could physically get out through it. The van sped through the complex so fast that I could see Neil Blaney and Sile de Valera, both on the hard bench opposite to me, sitting rigidly for fear of being thrown off as it rounded bends. I slid along my bench when the van screeched to a halt outside the hospital complex. We climbed down, glanced around us quickly and were herded inside.

The hospital complex had an hygienic atmosphere that greatly impressed me, and a silent lack of therapeutic intent that withered me. There were no relatives, no flowers, no suggestion that people were going to get better and get out. No hope. Clinically closed doors hid the scale of the misery. Four men had been transferred from the prison, buoyed up by cheering and singing from the other prisoners, but each of them was suffering the varied symptoms of starvation. Popular myth interprets starvation by choice as a relatively painless death; a gentle fading away from life. It is anything but. The agonies as the body's systems close down are unbelievable. One of the men now behind a closed door in this hospital was suffering stabbing pains the length of his body if he was touched. Sands had been given the last rites the previous Saturday. His skin was breaking down, and so he had to sleep on a sheepskin rug on top of a waterbed, and hospital staff rubbed him with cream every few hours. His eyes were hurting and he could no longer see properly.

150

Just before the member of staff opened the door of Sands's room, I told Sile and Neil that I was going to ask him to give up the strike. They said nothing, the door opened, and the three of us, well-dressed in our business suits, were ushered in to meet this dying man.

"You've got visitors, members of the European Parliament," said the warder.

I could not have expected Bobby Sands to look like the round-faced chubby boy in the posters, but the reality of how he currently looked was like a physical blow. I described him later to an artist for a newspaper and the newspaper did a drawing on the basis of my description which was accurate, but could not have the impact of the bone-white face and the physical stillness. He was skeletal. His eyes were glazed with the inattention of a man already focused away from the routine of daily living. I had little experience of starvation other than that provided by a few anorectic patients of mine, but I knew immediately that the emaciation was total and that irreversible physical damage had probably already taken place.

A member of the hospital staff stood at the door, but Sands seemed unaware of him, and we quickly forgot him. It was not a big room. A bed. A bedside locker with a radio on it. Food at the foot of his bed, on a trolley type table. Food and water. The constant unspoken invitation to give up, take just a bite.

He lay almost flat, just one pillow behind his head. On top of him, seeming to weigh him down, were sheets, a blanket and a cover. The cover was a brownish colour and the sheets were white. His face and the pillow lacked all colour. He was wearing a hospital gown.

I led the way into the room, walked around to the left hand side of the bed and took his hand. It was obvious that he had not the strength to lift it off the bed. By doctor's reflex I always take the pulse. He did not mind. It was a very thready pulse. Very weak. The hand ice cold, like touching a dead man. So cold I could not relinquish it, but held it gently in a vain effort to transfer warmth from my hand to his.

The air of death was inescapable, because here was a man who was barely able to talk. We had to lean down beside him to

151

hear him at times. Curiously, what brought a bit of animation to his face was a vague comment I made about the radio on the locker beside him.

"I suppose the radio keeps you up to date?" I asked.

"It did with the election results," he said, coming alive. "I was listening to the count."

It was a very strange thing. Although he had been terribly weak when we came into the room, with a barely audible voice, he then became quite lively, animated, and — yes, even happy. He talked. Told us about the hunger strike, why it had happened, what the five demands were and how they could be met by Britain without loss of face. He was clear in his thinking, resolute in his intention. While he talked, I moved a hand in front of his face and found that his wink reflex was already going. He seemed to me to have less than a week of life left him, and as a doctor I was primarily concerned to save that life. I asked him to give up.

"If you do give up the hunger strike we will fight to get the demands for the prisoners. Look, you've proved your point. You've proved your point."

He smiled at me silently.

"I knew you would say that," he said gently, and indicated that no, he would not be coming off the strike. Sile, who had watched my plea in silence although she would not have agreed with it, was clearly very moved and close to tears.

She held him very gently, so as not to hurt his sore skin, and kissed him.

Neil Blaney I had always seen as a strong man. He was very gentle on that occasion. You see a man in a different light when you see him supporting someone's republicanism, holding his hand gently, full of concern for him while not agreeing with my request to him to abandon the hunger strike. Sile and Neil both told him he was a hero. It was my turn to respect their position and be silent. All the conversation was quiet — not because of any desire to hide what was being said from the man at the door, but because Bobby Sands's voice was so low that the rest of us would have been deafening if we had talked at a normal pitch. Whispered voices and clinical hygiene and a conversation spinning between statements about patriotism to the death and a naive boy's delight over having become, *in absentia*, an MP. A very young man, gleeful about his first experience of politics and absurdly happy with his status as a parliamentarian. The voice grew stronger, and the phrases more fluent. The mouth moved in animation in his skull-like face, with lips so dry that every time he talked they cracked and the blood dried black on them.

I decided that we were wasting whatever physical resources he had, and that we should go. No prison or hospital staff made the suggestion. Their attitude was detached, respectful but uninvolved. I told him we would make a statement calling on Mrs Thatcher as a matter of urgency to save the life of this man by implementing the proposals of the prisoners. We stood. Neil Blaney touched Sands's face with infinite gentleness. I put my arms round him — his back was hard with unprotected bone. We left him, in no doubt that he was dying and that he would not stop the hunger strike in order to live. The parting was emotional, and Sile was in tears.

Out of the hospital building we went, to be re-loaded into the van and locked in all over again, as if visiting members of the European Parliament normally ran around prisons blasting their way into or out of cells. The men locking us in had no sense of the ridiculous, but then that happens in armies. Duty must be done and routine maintained, no matter how devastating the surrounding circumstances or how irrelevant the duty.

We were taken to Belfast, to a hotel where the newspaper people and the media men were. I particularly remember that just before we went into the hotel, Gerry Adams appeared around the corner.

"Look," he said. "I don't want to be seen with you in there — it wouldn't help you — but I did want to say thank you."

The meeting was all set up for us. Lights and flashing cameras everywhere. They were all very anxious to hear how Sands was and what was happening and was he going to die. They were concerned with the immediate thing. We were concerned with the demands of the prisoners. I called on Margaret Thatcher to respond to the demands — within an hour

153

her reply came and it was curt in the extreme. That night she made a statement from Downing Street saying that under no circumstances would she yield to any demands. I could scarcely believe it. She did not even deplore the loss of life which would follow inevitably on her decision to take no action. When we asked her to meet us, the answer was a crude negative.

"It is not my habit or custom," she said, "to meet MPs from a foreign country about a citizen of the UK, resident in the UK."

So that was it. A week later, Bobby Sands was blind and hearing noises in his head. He had constant stomach and chest pains.

On Sunday, May 3rd, 1981 he lapsed into a coma, and two days later he died. He was not the only one. Several of the men in the Maze went, one after the other. Cruel graffiti went up in Unionist areas saying "We'll never forget you, Jimmy Sands."
Reading about it in the Dublin newspapers sickened me, because there was just enough truth in it. Today, if you ask even ardent Republicans the names of those ten people, very few can remember more than one or two.

People in this country have great passions but very short memories.

# Chapter 8

# Starting Afresh

When I first thought about the possibility of becoming a member of the European Parliament, one of the major considerations putting me off the idea was my fear of flying. No minor discomfort this, but major terror. Having to travel in a small private plane with members of the IRA to meet Harold Wilson had paralysed me to such an extent that the subsequent relief made me go to sleep in the middle of the meeting. This, I decided, could not go on. It was something which had to be faced. I would have to learn everything about flying. I bought shelves-full of books about the basics, and read them with fearful devotion, gaining nothing but the technical terms for the processes that still terrified me.

The next logical step was taking flying lessons from Iona Airways. I know precisely how many I took: twenty. Each one is imprinted on my brain like a cerebral tattoo. I had one very good instructor who was most patient with me, because I would freeze in the plane, but as I progressed with the lessons, instead of him, I had a Yugoslav instructor who was much more assertively efficient. All speed and orders and action. No questions asked. Suddenly, I was out on the runway of Dublin Airport, planes (it seemed to me) flying in all directions.

"Pull that lever out," he said, pointing to it. "Go on. Pull it out. All the way. Yes. That's right. Now — see, you took off by yourself."

My reaction to this revelation was to beg him to take over the controls instantly.

Gradually, I became a little more at ease in a plane. I was helped by the fact that air crews on Aer Lingus flights were aware of my problem, and every time I went up, they would send for me, take me up to the cockpit and explain everything, which was extremely helpful and reassuring. Unfortunately, on one occasion when I was in Dublin Airport, a plane was delayed and a pilot who knew me spotted me and brought me off to see the controls of a plane on the apron.

"You see that lever," he said, in a way that was reminiscent of my Yugoslav tutor. "When you pull that, it sends you spinning down the runway."

I was comfortable, thus far.

"Then, when you get the speed up," he went on, "you pull the second lever."

I nodded.

"Of course, when you pull that," he said,"there's no going back."

That made me feel infinitely worse.

For a while, after I had become a Member of the European Parliament, I followed advice I had been given to stop being a teetotaller, and to take a drink before a flight. It would take the fear out of flying I was told. The problem was that, as a life-long teetotaller, I had no clue as to how to use alcohol. I would wait until the flight was due to take off, then grab a pint of Harp and drink it fast — glug-glug. The alcohol never seemed to have the smallest effect on my air phobia, but the moment I landed at the European destination, it would hit me, and during any meetings I attended, I would be fighting off grogginess. In time, I developed a touch of fatalism about flying. It did not totally remove the fear, but it never left me groggy...

The rationale that led me to Europe started in the seventies as I began to see more and more power usurped by Brussels and decisions being made over there which affected Ireland's future. By inference, Brussels was the place to be.

However, the first step was to study the European Parliament and how it worked. That resulted in my publishing a little booklet called *20 Questions on the European Parliament*. It also resulted in the decision to go forward for Europe.

Winning a seat in Europe propelled me into the hardest working phase of my entire political career, and into a period of near-invisibility. Getting the right to speak in the European Parliament, and getting what you said noticed, were twin problems which were neatly circumvented by a British MEP at the time, who copped on that even if he couldn't be permitted to speak in the European Parliament as often as he would like, he could still release a speech, datelined "Strasbourg" and half the relevant newspapers would carry it, assuming it had been made in the Parliament.

The same man went to Washington as a member of a European Parliament group. Realising that his chances of coverage over there were even smaller than in Strasbourg, he went to a function attended by the British Ambassador, who did not know him, and who, inevitably, did not greet him. The MEP promptly released a statement accusing the Ambassador of snubbing him, and got headlines in the British media as a result.

In spite of restrictions on speaking time in the European Parliament, I concentrated on health matters and consumer protection. I did manage to persuade the European Parliament to hold public hearings on consumer rights in Dublin, despite strong competition from Britain, Italy and Germany. I did it by promising things I was not at all sure I could deliver, including Dublin Castle as a venue. Having made the promise, I then went to Jack Lynch, the Taoiseach, to see if he would deliver on it which he did, and when Mr Haughey became Taoiseach, he followed through on that promise, agreeing, in addition, to officially open the Conference.

They came from all over Europe to it. MEPs. Consumer Groups. Journalists. So many of them that there was not enough room, and sections of Dublin Castle which were not planned as part of the venue had to be opened up to accommodate the overflow.

I was the *rapporteur*, and in that role, was to greet the Taoiseach when he arrived to open the Conference officially. By way of preparation for this important job, I had quickly bought an off-the-peg suit and dressed in it that morning. As I stood at the top of the stairs waiting for the Taoiseach to arrive,

I noticed a loose thread in the trousers and gave it a vigorous pull. From ankle to thigh, the inside seam opened neatly and irrevocably. There I was at the top of the stairs, the trouser leg free-floating like a flag unless I stood quite still and held it in place by the pressure of the other leg. When the Taoiseach arrived at the bottom of the stairs, he looked up at me. I stood still. He looked at me quizzically. I still stood still. He looked at me with growing irritation and indicated that I should come down the stairs. I stood still, silently begging him to come up the stairs to me, which he eventually did, mystified by my stasis. I went in and someone lent me a stapling machine. Clunk. Clunk. Clunk. In went the metal clips through the new fabric. Out they came again as soon as I walked. Someone gave me two safety pins and a tenuous connection was made between the two sides of my trouser leg. At lunchtime, I escaped for long enough to change into a much older, but more committed pair of trousers. When I later explained all this to the Taoiseach, it seemed to fit into a pattern in his mind.

Some months earlier, I had been in his rooms in the Dáil for a meeting with him, when he had momentarily become distracted from the subject in hand.

"John, do you know you're wearing odd shoes?" he asked.

I looked down. One brown. One black. Without a word, I backed out his door, grabbed an usher in a half-hearted attempt at personal concealment, and got out to my car through the back door of Leinster House. The next morning, when I mentioned to the journalists working with me in *Irish Medical Times* that I had spent a good chunk of the previous day walking around in odd shoes, one of them said that she had noticed me in them, but had assumed I had done it deliberately!

What I had planned to achieve, as a result of the Dublin Castle Conference which began so embarrassingly, was a Charter of Rights for Consumers. All of the consumer groups present were thrilled with the document which emerged. My next task was to put it through the European Parliament. That was when I saw Big Business in action. Big Business as represented by the Christian Democrats (the grouping to which Fine Gael is affiliated). All the way, they obstructed that

Charter of Rights and totally emasculated it.

"God," I thought desperately, watching what was happening. "If only the people who voted for these could see what they're doing."

And then I realised — Big Business had undoubtedly voted for them, that was what they stood for, and they did its bidding. All too efficiently, they did its bidding, killing off any form of legislation going through the European Parliament which would restrict their rights in any way. My Charter of Consumer Rights got nowhere. It never had a chance.

One of the things the European Parliament did for me was make me appreciate the latitude given to speakers in Dáil Eireann. In the Dáil, a member could speak for forty five minutes on something important. In the European Parliament, no matter how important the subject, I was lucky, as a member of one of the larger groups (the Socialists) to get five minutes. The Parliament is heavily biased towards giving time to Independents, with the result that people like Ian Paisley had virtually all the scope they ever wanted, whereas I found myself, on one occasion, doing a deal with another Member on the share-out of five minutes' speaking time between us. He started and took three minutes. I ended up with two minutes to outline the unemployment problem in Ireland — some task. On another occasion, I wanted to speak on the necessity of a health policy for Europe. I had initially to go before my own group, which included Barbara Castle and Ann Clwyd of the British Labour Party, a German ex-Minister for Health and a French member.

Surviving that gave me the right to speak in Parliament, seeking, first and foremost, standardisation of health services throughout Europe. But what I discovered was that the health services in European countries are mostly funded by private insurance and that the Irish health services were as good as if not better than their European counterparts with the notable exception of Britain.

Back on the home front, by early 1981, I had lost the possibility of running in the next election for the Labour Party, yet I was still in the Party. There is much talk today about "photo opportunities." Back then, there were "slagging opportunities" for Dr. John O'Connell. Journalists were fascinated by a Party that was preparing to run an election campaign without its best vote-getter, and so there was an open notebook or an open microphone awaiting my every negative word. Tempting. But pointless. It made a lot more sense to go and see Frank Cluskey, tell him I would resign from the Labour Party and shake hands on it. Which is what I did. There was no bitterness. A most amicable discussion. A final parting. After that final parting I did not feel I should attack the Labour Party again, nor did I.

Therefore, I ran for the 1981 election as an Independent. I concentrated on constituency work in the last months coming up to the election, meeting with a sympathy on the doorsteps I had not expected and which certainly contributed to my excellent showing at the polls.

The election was not a good one for Fianna Fáil, but no other party had anything close to a majority. After the inconclusive result I arranged to meet with the other Independents — people like Neil Blaney, Noel Browne and Thomas McGiolla— to see how we would approach the new Dáil that was about to be convened. The big problem facing everyone, the main parties and the Independents alike, was who would accept the position of Ceann Comhairle. Without a Ceann Comhairle there could be no Dáil, and no party would allow any of its own members to go forward for the job, as it would mean the loss of a seat. About one hour before that was due to happen, I had a telephone call from Jimmy Tully, asking me to consider becoming Ceann Comhairle. Michael O'Leary had taken over from Frank Cluskey as Leader, because Frank had lost his seat in that election, and Tully was O'Leary's emissary.

"Give me a few minutes to think about it," I said, and put down the telephone. The room was filled with my supporters, the people who have worked with me for years.

I told them what Tully had said.

"What do I do?" I asked them.

Go for it, they said. Take it. Without proper deliberation I went over to Leinster House at about five minutes to two to

160

accept, knowing that the new Dáil was meeting at 2.30. On the way, I encountered Peter Barry, who told me that I had been preceded by Sean Dublin Bay Loftus, new to the Dáil that Election, offering his services as Ceann Comhairle. However, the invitation having been extended to me, he met with a refusal. Garret FitzGerald formally proposed me as Ceann Comhairle, and a new Dáil got underway with the Coalition in power supported by Independents.

That Dáil lasted a mere six months from July 1981 to January 1982, with Garret FitzGerald as Taoiseach and with me in my new role as Ceann Comhairle. A failure in the job. Olivia O'Leary, writing in the *Irish Times*, described me as being like a spectator at Wimbledon, mesmerised by the play moving from one side to another in front of me. I hated the description, but it was absolutely correct. Summed it up perfectly. It wasn't easy to sit back and keep quiet on issues about which I felt strongly. Rather frustrating, I thought.

I knew the members and liked them and wanted them to have their say. Being too strict was not, I thought, a good idea. I was lenient. It did not work. It alienated the people I cut short, and it gave the people I allowed to talk, an impression that I was a soft touch.

In fact, however, it was the first independent action I took as Ceann Comhairle that most alienated opinion among the members of the new Coalition Government that had appointed me. That was on the second day in my new role, when it was time to elect the Leas Ceann Comhairle. I was nominated by Garret FitzGerald on behalf of the Coalition Government and seconded by Independent, Neil Blaney.

It had been the tradition in Leinster House for the Government to nominate the Ceann Comhairle and the Opposition to nominate the Leas Ceann Comhairle. This had gone on over the years, dating back, I was told, to the twenties, up until 1973 when Mr Liam Cosgrave changed it, nominating the Ceann Comhairle as well as the Leas Ceann Comhairle.

In 1977, Taoiseach Jack Lynch retaliated by appointing two Fianna Fáil men.

When it came to 1981, my close personal friend Paddy Harte

161

of Fine Gael was a candidate, as was Fianna Fáil TD Jim Tunney, who I barely knew. I had met Jim Tunney perhaps three times in my life.

On this occasion, I had a casting vote, and promptly cast it, not for my friend Paddy Harte, but for the Opposition candidate, Jim Tunney, explaining the reason for my decision to restore the status quo which had been broken by Cosgrave and Lynch. Paddy Harte never forgave me and Garret FitzGerald was enraged and never forgot it. But I felt that if I was my own man, this was what I had to do just as on a later occasion, when Charles Haughey was Taoiseach, he said something unparliamentary about a former Minister for Justice, and as Ceann Comhairle I objected and asked him to withdraw it. It's not often a Ceann Comhairle takes a Taoiseach to task!

Fine Gael seemed to see that initial casting vote against their wishes as putting me in the enemy camp, and whenever I allowed the Opposition time to ask innumerable questions, up would come the plaint from the Government side: "You're obstructing the progress of the House." But what is the progress of the House? The whole purpose of a TD in Opposition is to elicit answers to questions, and I felt it was my duty to give him (or her) as much rope as I could, to facilitate the Opposition as I would have wished to be facilitated in that role. Opposition members were there to question Government Ministers and to make Government answerable to the people.

Six months later, in January 1982, another election. It was the first election I did not have to fight. Another inconclusive result and difficult to predict which party would form the government. A phone call to me from Garret FitzGerald. I went to see him in his house. He was white in the face with exhaustion, having been up all night talking to various people in an effort to win the necessary majority to form the government and had failed. He looked very despondent and asked me not to go forward as Ceann Comhairle, on the basis that my refusal to take on the role would oblige the President to call in the various Party Leaders to make some kind of arrangement.

"Garret," I said. "we have to have a Ceann Comhairle. Not to have one would be irresponsible. It would be playing games with democracy. I couldn't do that."

That terminated the conversation.

Later that day Neil Blaney proposed me as Ceann Comhairle, I was seconded ("formally and warmly") by Garret FitzGerald, and I donned the ceremonial robes for a period lasting a further ten months.

During those ten months, there were eleven occasions on which I was called upon to use my casting vote. The last time before that when a Ceann Comhairle was called upon to give his casting vote was in 1935. The rule in relation to the casting vote is that the Ceann Comhairle must always give his casting vote in favour of the Government in power, because the Ceann Comhairle cannot be seen to be bringing down a Government. I therefore had no option but to support the Fianna Fáil government of 1982.

Although I was doing all of my constituency work, (a touch more efficiently than in the past, because I now had better secretarial support) my constituents were taken aback to find me in the position of a political eunuch. I could take no party political stance, nor could I attend any political meetings. There were bevies of advisers telling me what I could do and what I could not do.

But it was a time of political uncertainty, and after 10 months in November, 1982, Mr Haughey's Government fell. Garret came to me and told me he would not be proposing me as Ceann Comhairle on the basis that I had voted against him on the question of the Leas Ceann Comhairle.

When the Dáil reassembled in December 1982, he nominated the Fine Gael man Tom Fitzpatrick from Cavan as Ceann Comhairle and Labour's John Ryan as Leas Ceann Comhairle. In my first speech from the floor after a long absence, I made an impassioned plea to Garret to give the position of Leas Ceann Comhairle to Fianna Fail, (I was an Independent at this time) and so prove himself the great statesman so many of us believed him to be. My plea fell on deaf ears. And the fact that it did fall on deaf ears confirmed the gradual erosion of Garret FitzGerald's image in my mind.

So here we go again, I thought, as the Dáil began to take

shape. Or do we? I talked to people. I arranged coffee mornings and made brief presentations about what we needed to do about unemployment. Why couldn't we, I asked, rearrange things so that instead of paying people dole to be idle and demoralised, we paid that amount of money to an employer who would then top it up to a real living wage, and who would guarantee to do that for a year? I had several ideas along those lines, and groups of listeners would nod at me, pat me on the back, tell me I was a great man, and warn me that as an Independent I had no chance in hell of making those ideas reality. If I was to change anything, I had to join a political party. But which one? The Workers' Party?

Oddly, an oblique contact had been made with that Party when I was still Ceann Comhairle. One of the duties of the Ceann Comhairle is to meet an Ambassador as soon as he has presented his credentials to the President and has met the Taoiseach. So, when the Russian Ambassador arrived, he gave a reception for me in his house. I returned the compliment and had him to dinner. He telephoned again, and hosted another dinner. And a third. And a fourth. We would have long discussions about socialism, about social democracy, about the conditions here and about what should be done about them. He and his political assistant would talk about who was doing what for the country, and in the course of conversation, he would ask me about Sinn Fein, The Workers' Party. Why were they not receiving more support?

"I suspect that if they dropped the name Sinn Fein they might get more," I said.

Three weeks later, they dropped the Sinn Fein tag. I was surprised, and it seemed significant. When rumours began to surround me as an Independent, raising the possibility of my joining Fianna Fail (those rumours not emanating from me) I got a phone call asking me to meet the Ambassador's assistant for lunch.

"Don't tell me you're going to join Fianna Fail," he said at one stage. Since I was casting around in my mind but had made no decision, I simply shrugged. Within a fortnight, another phone call came, inviting me to lunch "with some other TDs". I accepted, but on the day, something happened to prevent me attending. I subsequently found that the other TDs present were all Workers' Party, so the assumption must be that this was to explore the possibility of my joining them. It had never been a runner, from my point of view. I had never liked the impression I had that the Workers' Party were taking their orders from someone else, and that when a Workers' Party man got up to speak, he had received directions and orders. Nor was I comfortable with their funding. But I had been very impressed with the way they supported me on the Griffith Barracks issue in 1965. When Labour refused to endorse my stand for the homeless it was Sinn Fein of Gardiner Place who stood by me and gave those families great support, even opening up their offices as temporary accommodation and providing blankets and hot meals for them when the families were flooded out on the site adjoining Mountjoy Square.

If I was still undecided, many of my constituents were not.

One woman in Walkinstown didn't put a tooth in it.

"For God's sake, Dr. John," she said. "You may have great ideas but no chance of putting them into practice. There's only one man will implement them for you and he's Charlie Haughey. Will you for God's sake throw in your lot with him?"

I went home that night and wondered if I was living in cloud-cuckoo land as an Independent.

Over the years, there had been much contact between me and Charles Haughey. There had been the occasions when he, using me as intermediary, almost met Ian Paisley. There had been the times during the various hunger strikes, when I had been in his house while he sought a solution.

On one holiday weekend I had been at his house while he tried desperately to get through to British Government Ministers, and had been deeply impressed by the relentless energy he was prepared to devote to a problem. At a time of high inflation, the Irish Congress of Trade Unions had demanded a 20% increase for social welfare recipients from Charles Haughey then Minister for Health and Social Welfare. I had sympathised with the demand, and been startled when he gave, not 20%, but 25% . There was a remarkable dearth of plaudits. When my good friend Bruce Arnold had written, in 1979, about Charles Haughey, then Minister for Health, that he was "of doubtful integrity," I had arranged for them to meet, because I felt that face-to-face, they would come to a better understanding.

I was a Labour Party deputy in December, 1979 when, while he was being elected Taoiseach, Charles Haughey had to sit through that remarkable speech of Garret FitzGerald's with the reference to a "flawed pedigree." The gallery was packed that day and he sat there quietly, listening. Over the years I had much contact with Charles Haughey. I have the habit of telling people what they should do, and I made no exception of him. He always listened. Sometimes he did what I felt he should do. Sometimes he absolutely refused.

I also had much contact, over the years, with Fianna Fáil people generally, and that contact had caused me to revise my opinion that Fianna Fáil was all about rich people. It was made up of teachers and clerks and ordinary people. It was the party that had made most provision for the poor, made some effort to create social balance, and straddled the political spectrum. Since Sean Lemass's time, it had consistently improved the social services.

I decided to join Fianna Fáil. Arrangements were made. I was to apply formally to join a Cumann. I did. I was received into the Cumann the night after a particularly controversial vote on the Contraception Bill. Received with a warmth that meant a lot to me. The next day, I went to the Fianna Fáil Parliamentary Party meeting and received a standing ovation.

It was the beginning of a new phase. When I joined Fianna Fáil we were in Opposition, and a Coalition Government dedicated to fiscal rectitude was in power. The tide was beginning to run against that Coalition, and within two years, a General Election was called. I was new to Fianna Fáil and its procedures. The Fianna Fáil people were new to me. My move had handed the other side a marvellous weapon, and they used it happily against me with the result that I lost my Dáil seat. A shattering experience after 22 years in the Dáil from 1965 to 1987. But while I thought my political life had come to an end,

Mr Haughey thought otherwise and promptly nominated me as a Senator.

# Chapter 9

# A Sort of Political Summing-Up

Dublin is a sweetly dangerous city if you're an energetic non-conformist. There's a warm approving tolerance for such people, best summed up in the phrase "Fair do's." Fair do's to your man all the same. You have to hand it to him. More power to him. Odd as two left feet, but one of our own.

It's a warm tolerance extended to "characters" like Forty Coats. It's extended to literary figures — as long as they drink and give lip to the Establishment. It's extended to political dissenters, especially if they are passionate, vocal and do not actually change things.

It frightens me, because I have felt the snuggling comfort of it. Leaving that comfort to join the majority political party, from my background and at this stage of my life, was riskier than going across the Atlantic single-handed on a skateboard.

When that party moved into Government and began to implement radical cost-cutting throughout the economy, the risk deepened. What happens to John O'Connell, fighter-from-the-sidelines, when he's part of a Government party — especially a Government which is clearly not in the business of soft options?

The short answer is, I don't know. The long answer is that I have never set out to be a lovable eccentric crusader, stroking ideals that have no prospect of being made to earn their living as realities. I have set out to make things happen. Most of them have not happened. This book is not a celebration of my successes; it's a litany of my failures. Dr. John can count his achievements on the fingers of one hand. He set out to change social structures and cycles of poverty. Social structures are largely unchanged, and cycles of poverty and desperation grind on, generation after generation, differing only in their outward symptoms.

In the old days, you had bed bugs, red raddle walls and TB. Today, you have head-lice, high rises and drugs.

I set out to control the brutal contempt with which all bureaucracies treat the poor, yet those bureaucracies have not been changed in their basic lack of respect for people. It's a curious irony that some of the most successful capitalist operations, whose key objective is to make profits, have specialised in being "customer-friendly" — in treating individuals of all classes with friendly respect — whereas many of the State-based agencies whose key objective is to serve the public, continue to treat their customers with unfriendly disrespect. It is a good thing that we have an Ombudsman, but there are thousands of people each and every year brutalised by their encounters with the national and municipal bureaucracies, who are not aware that the Ombudsman can have an impact on their problem.

That worries me. What worries me even more is to see people beaten into a sense of powerlessness, a conviction that this is the way things are, and that you cannot change them.

We have to change them. You shouldn't have to go to a McDonald's hamburger franchise in order to get a civil response or a smile. All state agencies that touch on the public — particularly on the disabled, the sick or the poor — should be pushed to deliver their services with greater courtesy, better communication, and greatly enhanced responsiveness.

That is one of the reasons I am now a member of a large, rather than a marginal party. As an Independent and, earlier, when I was a member of a small party, I had the idea that I could influence thinking towards change. I looked at men I admire, like Michael D. Higgins and Emmet Stagg, and waited for results from their totally committed activities. No results. I can no longer believe in the influence of the Outsider politician.

Large parties can change things, and large parties are rarely influenced by Independents, except in those once-in-a-political-lifetime circumstances when Independents happen to hold the balance of power. Therefore, it is important to be inside.

However, when you opt, as I did, to join Fianna Fáil from a quite different political background, it is widely assumed that you have made a radical change in the way you see things and people. In fact, I still admire the people I have always admired, whether in the Labour Party or in other parties. But liking people and admiring them has never stopped me fighting with them. One example is the Leader of the Party of which I am now a member. Charles J. Haughey is a man of formidable intellect, style and competence. I have seen him behave with great dignity when attacked, especially on one occasion when he was attacked in the Dáil in particularly personally hurtful terms, expressed with a vagueness that made rebuttal impossible.

I have also found him to be open and active as a Minister and as a Taoiseach. None of this has prevented me fighting with him. One of our more recent arguments saw a silence break out which lasted for three months. Then, one morning, I was told in my office that the Taoiseach was outside in his car and wanted to see me. I went down, sat into the back seat of the car and he reached across me and closed the door.

"Leinster House," he told the driver, and off we went. Effectively, I had been hijacked by the leader of my Party, and in the process, been taught a lesson; no matter how much you disagree with someone, you have to pick up relationships and move on when you have a shared objective. It is a hard lesson to learn if, like me, you are not just concerned about issues, but *obsessed* by them. I am obsessed by deprivation, unemployment and emigration, and so I cannot bear postponement or compromise.

We have solved this kind of problem before. 84,000 people emigrated in 1956. They just left the keys in the door and went off on the boat. In 1957, Fianna Fáil came back into office and got the country under control, managed the huge national debt of the time, got employment going again and many of those people came back. This can happen again. My concern is that it should happen fast, efficiently and with people, rather than statistics, centre-stage.

But then, I have always wanted to put people centre-stage, and sometimes, when I failed to do it, I have — later — been grateful. In 1975, for example, I was deprived of the Lord Mayoralty by a bit of fancy footwork within the Labour Party. At the time, I raged. Right now, I don't feel happy about the way it was done. But the fact is that the first thing I planned to do when installed as Lord Mayor was to throw open the Mansion to the homeless. If I had done it, the repercussions would still be going on. Most of the more controversial things I have envisaged in my life, I haven't done, because of situations like those which, in 1975, surround the Mansion House and its occupants.

Nevertheless, in political circles, I have been interpreted as dangerously mercurial and not amenable to party discipline, no matter what party I am in. A curious perception, this, in view of the fact that as a member of the Labour Party, I never once voted against them in the Dáil. On one occasion, when I had a motion down in Dáil Éireann that old age pensions should be tax free, the Labour Party made me vote against my own amendment, and I obeyed out of party loyalty. Never a vote against the party — I bit the bullet every time. Even when it came to repressive legislation, like the Criminal Justice Act, 1976. I had put down amendments and at the last moment was told that if I did not vote against my own amendment, I'd be booted out of the Labour Party. The feeling of déja vu was enormous when, on my first night as a member of Fianna Fáil, I had to vote against the Coalition Government's Family Planning Bill, with which I agreed. There can be no question about my capacity for team play, of loyalty to a party. But it will never be passive loyalty.

Nor will that loyalty make me perform with the pompous illogicality which has prevented so many governments from talking with terrorists at a time when talk might help progress to be made. Terrorists don't go away, and regarding them as

171

sub-humans who should not be acknowledged does not work. In Kenya, in the fifties, the Mau Mau were regarded as sub-human. Nobody was ever going to talk to them. Yet, not so long ago, a representative of the Mau Mau was met in Buckingham Palace by the Queen. On the death of Kenyatta, the Queen sent a personal representative to his funeral. Terrorism is a matter of scale and time. The atomic bomb in Japan was terrorism on a scale not seen before or since. But today's terrorists are tomorrow's figures of legitimate influence. It is important to bring them into the political arena sooner, rather than later. We should be encouraging them to contest elections. I do not understand the mentality of people who kill other people for a Cause. But they are a force to be reckoned with, not wilfully ignored.

Terrorists must be talked to. One of the worst results of the activities of the IRA over the last twenty years is that they have, in terms of world perception, absolved Britain of much of the guilt she deserves. Twenty years ago, the long-standing discrimination in the North was so clearly evident that Britain stood indicted in the eyes of the world for what she tolerated and what she carried out. It was visibly a situation akin of South Africa. North of the border, there was a form of apartheid, with the Catholics as second-class citizens. The IRA intervention took Britain off the hook.

However, while we seek to influence terrorists, we should also be seeking to change the factors that give terrorists a justifications and a breeding ground. I am a great believer in integrated education, and I believe that the segregated education of children in the North has perpetuated a system almost of race hatred, based on fear and mutual ignorance.

That was why, when the Pope was coming here to Ireland, I went to see Monsignor Alibrandi, the Papal Nuncio, and asked him if he would get the Pope to make a statement when he came here to the effect that because of the very unusual situation in the North of Ireland, not only would they favour integrated education, but they would actually promote it. He did not meet the suggestion with any degree of enthusiasm. I then went to Europe and got a letter through to the Pope by

172

other means in the Vatican. Sadly, nothing came of it.

Talking to terrorists in an effort to stop the killing is one of the things I've been proudest of. If I can do it in the future with some hope of success, I'll do it again. But then, that's the story of my life: a refusal to be "realistic" if realism means double-talk, lack of caring, avoidance of risk.

To hell with realism, if that's what it means. Life is too short and there are too many people out there with problems.

# APPENDIX

# IRISH REPUBLICAN PUBLICITY BUREAU

## COMMUNICATION TO MR. HAROLD WILSON, BRITISH PRIME MINISTER FROM THE LEADERSHIP OF THE REPUBLICAN MOVEMENT

Sir,

The Leadership of the Republican Movement ordered a unilateral suspension of offensive military action in Britain and Northern Ireland on December 22nd 1974. In doing so, we asked for a reciprocal response from the British Government and a reply to our Peace proposals given to Mr. Rees on December 19th by the Feakle churchmen.

After sustaining the suspension of operations for 26 days and proving our sincere desire for a lasting peace by the total absence of action on the part of our forces, we were unable to renew the order suspending operations for the following reasons:

(a) there was no satisfactory reply from the British Government to our Peace Proposals;

(b) the response on the part of H.M. Forces on the ground and the number of political prisoners released was meaningless to our people.

We therefore resumed a position of hostilities from January 16th, 1975. We also made it clear we were willing to engage in meaningful talks with the appropriate authorities to secure an honourable and permanent end to this conflict.

On January 18th, we received a request to make two representatives available for discussions in private with representatives of H.M.G. We did so and since then four meetings have taken place. We noted Mr. Rees' statement about "effective arrangements" being devised to ensure that a new truce would not breakdown. Accordingly, we gave our representatives twelve points (copy attached) which we consider necessary for the maintenance of a truce.

These points were discussed at length with H.M.G. representatives on Tuesday, 21st inst. A second meeting was arranged for the following day. Only one H.M.G. representative turned up for that meeting and he stated he was unable to continue discussions. We also noted Mr. Rees' statement of the 23rd inst., terminating dialogue with Provisional Sinn Fein.

We regret these developments and believe they will lead to a worsening situation. After nearly a month of genuine and sustained suspension of hostilities, we were unable to report any substantial progress to our Movement and people. We believe the adoption of our twelve points for a bi-lateral truce will break the present empasse and pave the way towards a permanent end to this age old problem.

We trust you, Mr Prime Minister, will give these points your consideration and forward a reply to us. On our part, we shall suspend all offensive operations in Britain from midnight, Monday 28th January, 1975. The adoption of the twelve points will result in a suspension of hostilities in Northern Ireland as well. We reiterate our sincerity to explore every avenue to secure an honourable and permanent end to this war.

24/1/1975